To Dearest Liz,
who keeps the faith and
spreads the peace in ways known
and unknown.   In Friendship,
                                Colman

Opening Minds, Stirring Hearts

The Peace Studies Class

COLMAN McCARTHY

PAGE PUBLISHING, INC.
New York, NY

First originally published by Page Publishing, Inc. 2019

ISBN 978-1-64424-234-6 (Paperback)
ISBN 978-1-64424-235-3 (Digital)

Printed in the United States of America

Also by Colman McCarthy

Disturbers of the Peace: Profiles in Nonadjustment (1973)
Inner Companions (1975)
Pleasures of the Game: The Theory Free Guide to Golf (1977)
Involvements: One Journalist's Place in the World (1984)
All of One Peace: Essays on Nonviolence (1994)
Solutions to Violence (Editor, 2001)
Strength Through Peace: The Ideas and People of Nonviolence (Editor, 2001)
I'd Rather Teach Peace (2002)
At Rest with the Animals: Thoughts Over Thirty Years (2008)
Peace Is Possible (Editor, 2012)
Baseball Is Forever (2014)
Teaching Peace: Students Exchange Letters with Their Teacher (2015)

On the cover, Bethesda-Chevy Chase High School Peace Studies students and guest speakers Lily Flores and Rev. Chuck Booker.

Dedication

For My Family: Far-Flung and Near-Flung

Contents

Preface

S INCE 1987, I'VE been privileged to be teaching peace studies courses at Bethesda-Chevy Chase High School in Bethesda, Maryland. The academic door was opened when I was invited to speak in the mid-1980s to a gathering of Montgomery County principals and assistance principals at a conference in St. Michaels, a resort town in Southern Maryland.

Much of my talk was a call to create courses in alternatives to violence in the county's two dozen high schools. And in whatever form the violence is found: military violence, domestic violence, economic violence, environmental violence, emotional violence, racial violence, homophobic violence, verbal violence, handgun violence, assault weapon violence, corporate violence, religious violence, self-inflicted violence, prison violence, sexual violence, obstetrical violence, police violence, sports violence, legal violence, illegal violence, factory-farm violence, schoolyard-bully violence. If we keep urging our children to go out and make the world a better place, a peaceful place, why aren't we exposing them to the history, practitioners, and successes of nonviolence? If we don't teach our children peace, someone else may teach them violence.

Among the principals receptive to the idea was Nancy Powell of B-CC. The problem, she said, was none of her faculty was available to teach that kind of course—not in the school's political science department or the sociology department. "How about you?" she asked.

At the time, I was nearing my twentieth year as a syndicated columnist for *The Washington Post*, and with some of that time wondering why peace education had little or no place in American high schools. I had already been teaching as a volunteer of a weekly Literature of Peace class for five years at the School Without Walls, a progressive haven in Washington served by a stellar faculty. It was also the closest school to the White House, five blocks east. Walls, housed in a brick structure built during the Grant administration, was also one of the poorest schools in the country. It lacked a cafeteria, lockers, athletic fields, an auditorium, and, for a time, clean drinking water. President after president had been invited to speak at Walls, a quick jaunt away, but none ever came. Nor did their children. The Obama daughters were enrolled at the private and well-cloistered Sidwell Friends five miles away, not Walls five minutes away. The President's heart was in America's public schools, he assured us, but not his children.

To Nancy Powell's question—are you a talker or a doer, really?—I said I'm coming, and I don't need to be paid. I had many inspiring teachers growing up on the North Shore of Long Island who I could never repay for their help. So I'll pay my students what I owe my teachers.

In the early years, and in the sociology department to which seasoned teachers seemed to gravitate, I taught a first-period class that began at 7:25 a.m. Then, delighting in the intelligence and spirited ways of the students—all were seniors taking the course as an elective—I added a second period. I would finish at nine and be home by nine thirty and on my way to *The Post.*

Home was 4.5 miles south from B-CC, in American University Park. The round-trip commute was a daily nine miles—or forty-five miles a week, which in a forty-week school year tops out at 1,800 annually on my trusty Raleigh 3-speed. The joyriding legwork of 1,800 miles for three decades totals up to 54,000 miles. In addition to the free-wheeling physical benefits, bicycling has spiritual ones: rolling along unhurriedly, much of it on the uncluttered early dawn sidewalks by Wisconsin Avenue, and a chance to meditate on what matters in life. Moments arise to agree with Iris Murdoch: "The bicycle is the most civilized conveyance known to man. Other forms of transport grow daily more nightmarish. Only the bicycle remains pure in heart."

At B-CC, I've cherished my students too much to ever inflict them with homework, tests, or exams. These drudgeries are the plasticity of fake education. Students, self-pressured, tend to comply out of fear: obey my teacher's demands for homework and ace my tests and exams, or I might end up in a third-tier college.

No evidence exists that A's on a report card make you a kinder person, a gentler person. I try to remind my students of Walker Percy's line, you can make all A's in school but go on to fail at life. I've had more than a few classes in which I asked students to raise their hands if they are in a state of anxiety. Nearly all hands rise.

I fret about students who have 4.0 GPAs. What life experiences are they missing out on while grinding away for high grades? Instead of fear-based learning, I've preferred desire-based learning: anxiety-decreasing, not anxiety-raising education. Tension levels can rise, especially for seniors writing college-admissions essays and hoping they are sufficiently spiffy. Next is toting the extracurriculars and community service hours that can buff one's application to impress the anonymous gatekeepers, whether at the Ivies, Little Ivies, or Poison Ivies.

Without overdoing it but also trying to lower anxieties, I offer the idea that other GPAs exist, ones that last well beyond the school years: Give Parents Affection, Gentle People Affirm, Goodness Prevails Again, Go Practice Ahimsa, Grouches Provoke Aggravation and—here's my favorite—Goofs Putter Along.

Among the nation's teachers, I can't imagine that I'm alone in seeing grading students as degrading. For me, it's true whether I'm at B-CC or the other five classrooms I'm in with seven courses: Georgetown Law, Georgetown undergraduate, American University, and the University of Maryland. Grademongering prevails. For some driven students, anything less than an A is seen as a failing grade. I recall a B-CC mother phoning to ask how her daughter was doing in my class. "How would I know? I'm her teacher," I answered. That didn't help much, with the mother demanding to know the grade— and from the tonal tension in her voice, it better be an A. I quoted

Walker Percy, which assuredly didn't nail it. Finally I counseled the mother the best way to learn how her daughter was doing in the class: ask her.

It's worth remembering that two of history's most enduring teachers—Socrates and Maria Montessori—never assigned grades nor homework. Which prompts a question: who knows more about education, Socrates and Montessori or the average American school board? Guess.

"One should seek out an audience that matters," Noam Chomsky wrote. "In teaching, it is the students. They should not be seen merely as an audience but as part of a community of concern in which one hopes to participate constructively. We should be speaking not to but with. That is the second nature of any good teacher, as it should be to any writer and intellectual as well. A good teacher knows that the best way to help students learn is to allow them to find the truth by themselves. Students don't learn by a mere transfer of knowledge, consumed through rote memorization and later regurgitated. True learning comes about through the discovery of truth, not through the imposition of an official truth. That never leads to the development of independent and critical thought. It is the obligation of any teacher to help students discover the truth and not to suppress information and insights that may be embarrassing to the wealthy and powerful people who create, design and make policies about schools."

To help get a taste for independent and critical thought, as well as enliven the mornings, I've been inviting guest speakers to my classes. Washington, Bethesda, and Chevy Chase are flush with a varicolored mix of activists, not including those passing through the capitol. In the past three decades, more than four hundred of every stripe have generously given their time to come to the classes.

Many were former peace studies students, some returning like natives, others like prodigals. Many were parents and grandparents. All were women and men committed to use their moral and intellectual gifts incandescently. Among the four-hundred-plus were capitalists, socialists, communists, Democrats, Republicans, Libertarians, Greens, militarists, internationalists, humanists, theists, atheists, traditionalists, nonconformists, environmentalists, theorists, anarchists, and pacifists. They were Nobel Peace Prizes laureates—Adolfo Perez Esquivel, Mairead Corrigan, and Muhammad Yunus. They were exonerated death row inmates. Vietnam, Iraq, and Afghanistan war veterans. Corporate lawyers and public interest lawyers. Sentencing judges and sentenced defendants. Police officers. Alcoholics, warholics, peaceholics. Nurses, midwives, doctors, scribes, chefs, lobbyists. Farmers, landscapers, CEOs and COs, millionaires, thousandaires, and a sidewalk panhandler. Pastors, rabbis, priests, imams, nuns, monks. Buddhists, Hindus, Islamists, tribal chiefs. Blacks, whites, gays, straights, and transgenders. Peace Corps, AmeriCorps, VISTA, and City Year volunteers. Dissidents from the left and right. Members of Congress including Chris Van Hollen, Connie Morella, Andy Jacobs, Elizabeth Furse, and Pat Williams. Former major-league ballplayers like Pepe Frias The well-known: George Pelacanos, Rita Braver, Tim Shriver, Mark Shriver. Olympians, Special Olympians. Psychiatrists, janitors, B-CC alums. The scorned and silenced, the homeless and luckless. Sufferers of depression. Some riding high, others happy just to be hanging on.

I've been forever touched at the generosity of so many citizens who have come to share their thoughts and passions with the B-CC students—plus their energetic willingness to rise at predawn to arrive at the school for the first class at seven forty-five. For a decade, it was seven twenty-five. A prevailing belief during the visits in the class is that even if we don't see eye to eye, we can always speak heart to heart.

During the inevitable Q&As, which I encourage, the most rousing times have been not only when students ask questions but when they question the answers. Especially mine, and especially when I reveal my political leanings, my pacifist beliefs, what I stand for or stand against. I recall the time that Howard Zinn came to the class. He was in Washington to speak about his latest book, *You Can't Be Neutral on a Moving Train*. In it are some lines of quiet passion that were Howard's intellectual markings: "When I became a teacher, I could not possibly keep out of the classroom my own experiences. I have often wondered how so many teachers manage to spend a year with a group of students and never reveal who they are, what kind of lives they have led, where their ideas come from, what they believe in, or what they want for themselves, for their students, and for the world. In my teaching I never concealed my political views: my detestation of war and militarism, my anger at racial inequality, my belief in democratic socialism, in a rational and just distribution of wealth. This mixing of activism and teaching, this insistence that education cannot be neutral in the crucial issues of our time, this movement back and forth from the classroom to the struggles outside by teachers who hope their students will do the same, has always frightened the guardians of traditional education. They prefer that education simply prepare the new generation to take its place in the old order, not to question that order."

The morning after the visits from the speakers, we have a liturgy of peace studies gratitude: letters of appreciation to each of them.

What follows in these pages are the biographies of the speakers and a sampling of the thank-you letters. Together, they tell a story of high school students shining their lights, from the brightness of their idealism to the glow of their commitments to be peacemakers in ways small or large. They are students who have had their minds opened and hearts stirred by the speakers. The letters reveal an awareness that the way to make a difference in the world is to start to be different, to be daring enough to break away from the conventions and complicities that can stagnate much of our politics and culture. Some letters center on students knowing that they have won the birth lottery, being born into privileges common to the Bethesda and Chevy Chase communities, and wondering what might be owed for being among the fortunate. Still, other students candidly reflect on being unsettled on whether they will have the inner resilience to meet the expectations of their parents. Some wonder which obstacles may lie in their paths, forgetting that if your path has no obstacles, it may not be leading anywhere. The diversity of the students ranged from ones raised in Chevy Chase mansions to those whose parents immigrated from Bangladesh and Ethiopia.

Many students, overscheduled and academically overworked, find themselves pressured by the education-industrial complex pushing select courses and downplaying others. STEM is the latest wind gusting through high school hallways: science, technology, engineering, math. A CEO of a Silicon Valley tech company wrote in a letter to the editor of *The New York Times* on August 15, 2016, that "STEM education is more than supporting young people to become scientists and engineers." It is about "expanding the bounds of possibility and enabling students to make lasting contributions in any job." The same can be said about the humanities and the social sciences, except that students are not conned into believing that the purpose of life is making gobs of money and STEM is the tailwind to get it. I prefer STEPS—sociology, theology, ethics, peace studies—as the educational means to getting close to the truth found in the lines of Wendy Schwartz: "To find the way to make peace with ourselves and to offer it to others, both spiritually and politically, is the most important kind of learning. To accept our abilities and limitations, and the differences of others. This is the contentment that gives life its highest value. It frees us to grow without restraint and to settle without pressure."

At the end of each semester, fall or spring, and before wishing my students well—yes, peacemakers, go out and change the world but make sure the world never changes you—I take some moments for a reading from Albert Schweitzer's "Reverence for Life." This essay on idealism has nourished me often, especially when the off-ramp beckons to escape the fast lanes of life's absurdities: "No one has the right to take for granted his own advantages over others in health, in talents in ability, in success, in a happy childhood or congenial home conditions. One must pay a price for all these boons. What one owes in return is a special responsibility for other lives."

As the booned students leave, I look at them and wonder which ones I will remember, which ones I will hear from as the years pass, which ones will never waver from believing that the good life is incompatible with the violent life, which ones will remember me, if at all, as a teacher who wanted only to rouse their passions for justice and rally their gifts for peacemaking, and which ones will return to the class with narratives of life after high school and proving that every life is worth a novel.

It's a safe guess that in an era of e-mails, tweets, smartphones, iPhones, apps, Instagram, texting, Snapchat, and laptops, handwritten letters—actually fingering a pencil or pen over a piece of paper—are singular experiences for many students. Several embraced the moment, writing graceful and heartfelt prose written as a first draft and with no chance for polishing. The letters became palettes on which the students could paint their dreams and hopes of joining the ranks of the speakers, whether they were describing their work as prison reformers, hypnobirth counselors, public interest lawyers, mindfulness teachers, neonatologist doctors, recovering Vietnam veterans, or homeless survivors. When a speaker spoke about, say, the high cost of childbirth and the soaring rate of C-sections or the predominance of blacks on America's death rows or the victimization of students in Indian boarding schools or that more than six million animals are killed for food every hour worldwide in slaughterhouse and factory farms, or the squandering of billions of dollars for the America's ceaseless and useless wars, or the millions of civilians killed in them, or the economic violence of high-cost college tuitions, students wondered why they hadn't been exposed to these realities before now. They felt cheated, justifiably so. Often, they felt as if they were being processed like slabs of cheese enrolled in Velveeta High, on the way to Mozzerella U and Cheddar grad school.

Too well, students may connect with Carol Rinzler's lines in *Your Adolescent: An Owner's Manual*: "Little Kimberly asks her parents, 'If they tell you in nursery school that you have to work hard so you'll do well in kindergarten, and if they tell you in kindergarten you have to work hard so you'll do well in high school, and if they tell you to work hard in high school so you'll get into a good college, and assuming they tell you in college that you have to work hard so you'll get into a good graduate school, what do they tell you in graduate school that you have to work hard for?' Kimberly's parents answer: 'To get a good job so you can make enough money to send your children to a good nursery school.'"

Nearly all the speakers and the letters came during the fall and spring semesters from 2015 to 2018. Throughout the three years, I found myself thinking more than once that something special is going on, a rarity and a blessing that could well empower us to heed the advice of Melody Beatty: "Speak your truth. Listen when others speak theirs too. When you let go of fear, you will learn to love others, and you will let them love you. Open your heart to love, for that is why you are here."

Colman McCarthy
Center for Teaching Peace
Washington, DC

1

AMY HARFELD WAS in my peace studies class in 1990. The
year before, she was among the thirty students who came on our
field trip to death row in the Mecklenburg State Prison in Southern
Virginia. Besides the warden, our host was Joe Giarratano, an inmate
who conducted a seminar for the students on the arbitrariness of capital punishment. Within a year, Joe's death sentence would be waived
by Gov. Douglas Wilder who said he had "grave doubts" about the
prisoner's guilt. During lunch with Joe and the inmates, Amy learned
that many of the men lacked lawyers for their appeals, a violation
of the Sixth Amendment. Virginia supplies one public defender for
one appeal. After that, do it yourself—even though it is often on the
second and third appeals in which new DNA evidence is found, wit-
nesses recant, or prosecutorial deceits are uncovered.

Being denied a lawyer is wrong, thought a rankled and upset
Amy. Before the trip, she was something of an academic floater whose
interests focused more on what to wear than on what to think. The
death row visit jolted her, to the point that she came down to earth—
especially the large part of it beyond the safely cloistered Bethesda
and Chevy Chase. She threw herself into her studies and did well
enough to be accepted at the University of Michigan. There she double majored in criminology and women's studies. Graduating summa
cum laude, she went on to serve three years with Teach For America
at a low-income middle school in Compton, California. While there,
she did what few teachers ever do: routinely visiting the homes of
her students, there to witness the impoverishments likely to make

the students' future lives bleak and strengthen her resolves to prevent that. At one apartment the door was opened by a student with burn marks over his arms, the result of child abuse by a parent who put out his cigarettes on the boy's skin.

Witnessing as well as feeling the results of policies and legislation that did little to ease the victimization of her students, Amy believed she'd have a better chance of turning it around by becoming an attorney.

Accepted at several high-tier law schools, including Georgetown, Amy chose to get her JD at the City University of New York—a scrappy enclave that specializes in public interest law.

Amy, who spent a year on a kibbutz in Israel and is fluent in Hebrew, is currently a staff attorney in the Washington office with the Children's Advocacy Institute. Much of her work is lobbying Congress to pass legislation that would balm the wounds suffered by large numbers of the nation's four hundred thousand foster children. Amy, married to an Israeli, is the mother of Dalia and Gideon. As with many others who met Joe Giarratano in prison, she was heartened when he was paroled in December 2017 after thirty-eight caged years and now living in Charlottesville, Virginia, and working at a law firm.

Dear Amy:

As a teenager, I care so much and know so little. I consider myself to be an activist but beyond raising awareness and money for issues I care about, I don't know if I'm really doing much. I don't feel like I am as knowledgeable about the things I get angry about as I should be.

You showed me an example of someone who channeled he empathy into a profession, someone who knew what they were talking about and how to make a difference. I want to be like you! Your talk made me consider following a selfless path of fighting for those who don't have a voice for themselves.

Thank you for doing what you do and for inspiring all of us.

Much love,
Sophia Navratil

Dear Amy:

As someone who lives with incredible amount of privilege, it can be easy for me to forget the challenges others face on an everyday basis. As someone who grew up in Bethesda, I'm sure you are more than aware of the uniqueness of our school and town—the wealth, the virtually unquestioned assumption that you will finish high school and go to college, the privilege of living with connections and resources.

Your work, however, is a reminder of the importance of recognizing this privilege and using it to help others. Your commitment to bettering the lives of students and foster children is truly admirable, and as someone who wants to work in education policy, your work allows me to believe in the power and importance of thoughtful legislation and devotion to a cause, especially one that often seems hopeless

Thanks for exemplifying so clearly and courageously the power we have to make changes and benefit those who need it most.

Sincerely,
Eliza Braverman

Dear Amy:

Mr. McCarthy has told us so much about you, so I was especially excited to hear you speak. You surely did not disappoint. Your drive and determination to stand up for those who cannot stand up for themselves is inspiring. I am thinking about attending law school, and your story and advice reminded me to study something close to my heart and am passionate about.

I don't know how I would have reacted after finding a student of mine at home covered in cigarette burns, but you responded justly: by helping not only that one child but the countless others like him. Those children are so fortunate to have someone like you who will stand up and fight for them and against all the corruption and apathy in Congress.

One day I hope to be as dedicated, passionate, and committed to my job as you are. Maybe one day we can give a joint talk in Mr. McCarthy's peace studies class.

Sincerely,
Cate Paterson

Dear Amy:

I only heard you speak for an hour or so, but you have become such an inspiration and a reminder that there are people out there who are doing social justice as a job and who truly believe in change and not give up the fight.

What I kept turning over in my head the most is that you turned down those big-name law schools and what could have been a lucrative career, and consciously chose the path your heart was already taking. I try to care less about things that don't matter and more about the things that do, but I can only hope to have the dedication you do.

There must be so many difficulties and trials too, but first litigating for children and then actually lobbying for long-term change should like the absolute dream job, and I would be interested to know how you got to be where you are. I too have started planning for the service I will do after undergrad. I have been researching Peace Corps requirements and qualifications, but now Teach For American is definitely on my radar. But how did you get to represent children after law school? That seems like the kind of rewarding job many people would want.

Anyways, back to the cause. I think the work you do is effective a thousandfold because helping children also affects all the people they will grow up to be as adults. I have read many stories about a person recalling that one teacher who changed his or her life as you have done.

Thank you,
Mian Osumi

Dear Amy:

As a freshman this fall at Michigan who hopes to be a social justice lawyer, hearing you speak to my class was inspiring. I can only hope to graduate at the top of my class like you. Every time I read or learn about a new social justice issue, I feel a fire in my stomach and to fight for that issue. I am not sure which one will be my eventual focus, but now I will make sure to apply to City University for law school.

Thank you for fighting for those without a voice with no benefit to yourself, and thank you for spending your time teaching us about the discrepancies many of us were unaware of. I appre-

ciate it and hope to talk to you again soon about following in our footsteps.
Go Blue!

Sincerely,
Sabine Rundlet

Dear Amy:

I found your presentation positively impressive. Your entire career path and life sounds like a wonderful journey, and I had no idea that it could be launched by Mr. McCarthy's class.

Your commitment to public service and helping those who can't help themselves is inspiring, and though it is not the path I will choose I still look up to it and hope to have as active a career as yours.

Thank you,
Danny Roberts

2

N EEDINESS ISN'T THE first word that comes to mind when thinking about Mark Shriver. Born into relative wealth in 1964 as the abundantly loved fourth child of Sargent and Eunice Kennedy Shriver, he had a sterling Jesuit education at Georgetown Preparatory School in North Bethesda, Maryland, and the College of the Holy Cross in Worcester, Massachusetts. He enjoyed summers sailing off the Cape Cod coast of Hyannis Port with his uncle, Senator Ted Kennedy in his yawl *The Curragh*. On the expansive and rolling lawn of his parents' Maryland home, he played games with his brothers, sister, and multiple cousins. He married his college sweetheart, Jeanne Ribb, and became the father of Molly, Tommy, and Emma. He found meaningful work as president of the Save the Children Action Network to which he commuted from his home in Bethesda.

Despite the confluence of all these blessings, he was needy. Spiritually needy: "I had been yearning for a Church I could believe in again. How many times over beers had my buddies and I lamented the disconnect between the church hierarchy and the foot soldiers, the self-sacrificing nuns and priests serving the poor all over the globe. I had been needing my Church and my faith (the two, no matter how hard I tried, are as inseparable for me as they are for many Catholics) more than usual."

The lines are from Mark's 2016 book, *Pilgrimage, My Search for the Real Pope Francis*. In well-honed prose grounded in both reporting from Buenos Aires and devouring the writings, sermons, and papal documents, Mark found in Jorge Mario Bergoglio and his commitments to mercy and justice the kind of spiritual nutrients he needed and wanted.

Mark's visit to the peace studies class blended personal stories about his family, his faith and spirituality, and his professional work to end the violence inflicted on children to the point that sixteen thousand die every day from preventable diseases as well as eight hundred women who die daily from childbirth.

Dear Mark Shriver:

I was so fascinated to hear about the angelic work of you and your family. I have never heard of one that is as dedicated to humanitarian work. Education for young children is truly the first step to closing the education gap between those who are fortunate enough to grow up in an upper- or middle-class household as against those who up less economically secure.

As a practicing Jew, I am embarrassed to say that I don't know much about Pope Francis. Though I am fascinated by religion, I had not yet taken any time to research this widely respected yet controversial figure. As a result I was shocked and intrigued by the unpredictable path Francis has taken.

Now I am captivated by your research and writing. I absolutely want to read and learn more. There is no one more respectable, in my opinion, than a person who can see past sin or social standing and understand the personhood underneath.

Thank you for enlightening me. And thank you for the amazing and admirable work you are doing to ensure a moral, equal, and peaceful society.

Sincerely,
Celia Goldfarb

Dear Mark:

I am Catholic, so I enjoyed hearing about your journey to learn more about Pope Francis. I am going to recommend your book to both my parents. I think they would enjoy it.

I understand that the issues regarding children's education across the nation are a bit abstract to me because I've lived in Chevy Chase my whole life, but through listening to you, I also realize that I can still help. I will definitely try to talk and listen to homeless people and be more charitable toward them.

I pray to God that when I am older I can have a job as meaningful as yours.

Best,
Jillian Walsh

Dear Mr. Shriver:

I am not Catholic. I am not even Christian, but I have respect for people who selflessly help others whether it be from religion or something else. Your stories of the pope were completely astounding to me, someone whose knowledge of the pope peaks at the pope mobile, and the fact that many have had the same name. I could really see the unusualness of this pope with your many stories.

I admire the lengths you went to achieve your goal. It shows how a simple conversation can help me in a huge way.

I want to thank you for coming to our class, but more so I would like to thank you and your family for all they have done to improve our nation. I am lucky to have received the educa-tion I have and fully believe everyone should have access to learning. If the answer to many of our country's issues is early education, I support resources going to that cause.

Thank you again for all you have done. You have inspired me to use the privileges I have to help others.

Yours,
Dani Seltzer

Dear Mr. Shriver:

Your talk and your stories about the pope really got me thinking about how I treat the poor, specifically the homeless people who live around my apartment building. It's difficult, however, because as a girl I always have to be aware of my safety: my fear of being harassed plays into my lack of eye contact with the homeless men sitting by the bus stop.

But it's not supposed to be easy, is it? It's not supposed to make me comfortable, but I'd like to hear your thoughts.

It's amazing the opportunities you found in Argentina and finding people who knew the pope. He's a good man. I'm not Catholic but I'm a big fan of his.

You're a good storyteller. Thank you for coming.

Natalie Tomeh

Dear Mark:

The work that you and your family has done over the years is amazing in its breadth of purpose and impact. Each member of your family seems to have covered at least one distinct and unique area in which care and love are the top priorities. For example, the work your mother Eunice and brothers Tim and Anthony have done for the disabled in creating and maintaining the Special Olympics and Best Buddies without a doubt contributed enormously to help better the lives of the physically and mentally disabled.

You yourself have clearly accomplished amazing feats, from your time in the state legislature to your two books to your efforts to improve early education. Unfortunately, I have not yet spent much time researching and trying to understand the policies of early education, which I think reflects pretty accurately the general atmosphere of the country regarding this.

I am infinitely grateful that you have chosen to become one of the brave few to take on the government on this issue. I was especially amazed by your work at Save the Children Action Network and your success researching Pope Francis. Despite my irreligiosity and my general opposition to the Catholic Church, it still remains a powerful force in the world. I am glad that such a great man is at the head of it. He symbolizes a rare concern for those less fortunate than ourselves.

Thanks so much for taking the time to come speak to our class. I wish you great luck in your good works.

Sincerely,
Conor Smythe

Dear Mr. Shriver:

Hearing you speak yesterday touched my heart and soul. Listening to you, I felt fascinated and inspired by your work with Save the Children Action Network and your dedication to your faith.

Your stories about Pope Francis's compassion and humility intrigued me and I hope soon to read your book about him. Learning that sixteen thousand children and eight hundred mothers die every day due to preventable illnesses really opened my eyes to how much work still needs to be done for children and families in both America and around the world.

I am truly grateful to have been given the chance to hear you speak because it opened my eyes to not only the good and beautiful but also how much more effort and change needs to happen to improve our world.

Sincerely,
Elizabeth Mulvihill

3

NO FORMER PEACE studies student has ever returned to speak so authoritatively, or so engagingly, as Jacob Levin on acorns: how to find, cook, and happily eat them. No speaker, either, has ever earned a degree from rarefied Williams College that included a year among the dons at Oxford University and then decided, after making decent wages in a semisuffocating corporate cubicle, to break free and take up small-scale farming in North Carolina. What Jacob, whose sister Hannah came after him as a peace studies student, was unable to learn among the wise ones at Williams and Oxford—the arts of sustainable agriculture, crop rotation, herbal remedies, simple living, foraging, scavenging, and, yes, the gustatory delights of nutritious acorns—he learned on his own. The agrarian life, far from the anxieties, strivings, and noises of urban living, has left Jacob ample time for reading the kind of literature—philosophy, theology—he couldn't in college because of the usual academic strictures. Jacob sprinkled his remarks with allusions to philosophers, theologians and ethicists—most of whose ideas he learned on his own, as he did by self-educating himself about small-scale farming. Jacob is in a long of renegade earth-loving spirits like Henry David Thoreau, John Muir, Scott and Helen Nearing, Wendell Berry, and Woody Guthrie (think "This Land is Your Land").

> Dear Jacob:
>   Until yesterday I never knew humans could
> use acorns as a source of nutrition. After taking

AP Environmental last year, I was able to understand exactly what you were talking about and the terms you used. The work you are doing now is cool, and I hope that you will reach your goal of owning and operating your own farm—and a farm with as much biodiversity as possible because it is really important. I also hope that in the future all new buildings will be required to have green space or an aquaponics system on their roofs. I hope for the future!

Thank you again!

Katie Weber

Dear Jacob:

I really enjoyed hearing about your life yesterday, especially when you described how to prepare and eat an acorn. I am currently taking AP Environmental Science, and I have learned a lot about farming and living sustainably.

Your story is inspiring because you drastically changed your life to do what you love. We need more people (and farmers) like you.

Thank you for coming in.

Sincerely,
Jenna Troccoli

Dear Jacob:

You were the first speaker to come into our peace studies class this year. You could have been anyone—a war veteran, a congressman—but I'm glad it was you who we got to listen to: a self-proclaimed scavenger, a man who is brave enough to go off the beaten path and do what is right for the future of this earth even if it's not the most popular preference.

That you were raised and grew up in such a similar environment as me is what really makes me admire your story. I've been thinking a lot recently about how important it is to do what makes me happy, to do things because I want to do them, not because someone else wants me to.

At a turning point in my life (high school graduation, college, future decisions) I'm thankful that you were here to inspire me to follow my heart.

Sincerely,
Katy Vicenzi

Dear Jacob:

You are one of the most interesting people I have ever had the pleasure of listening to. It's inspiring that you lived your life like we did but decided to make your life better by escaping the "Bethesda Bubble." The way you approach life is fascinating, and I think it is so cool how you still consider you are a student. I am so impressed with how you live your life. Your comments really made me think about my own life and what is really important to me. I feel like a lot of adults just stop learning after grad school, college, whatever.

Thank you so much for coming in.

Mallory Mical

Dear Jacob:

I think it's safe to say that you know more about acorns than anyone I know. That might just be my nature deficiency disorder talking, but I really enjoyed having you as a speaker in our class. I appreciated your comments about increasing biodiversity and avoiding hydrological fracturing. It's pretty messed up how many species humans have been destroyed—plants and animals. Thank you so much for coming to our class.

Best,
Eve Chesivoir

Dear Jacob:

When you came into my peace studies class, I felt a renewed sense of hope in the human race. Thanks you so much for speaking to us about your way of life, and how you came to be after B-CC. I have always felt passionate about environmental and food-industry issues, so much so that I started a tree protest here last week (on the school's front lawn). Pepco was trying to cut down a perfectly good tree! I also bother my grandma about buying local foods. I love that you made a way of life for yourself that is so unique and so brave. I would love to try your acorn chili. It sounds so fascinating. Maybe you can come back to visit and bring some.

I hope that I find a path as you did and become so sure of myself.

Thank you.

Lillian Wessel

Dear Jacob:

I went home yesterday and researched a gap year. I've known for a long time that I want to be a surgeon, but your talk made me want to take a step back and explore all my options before I dive into another ten years of school. I think it's absolutely incredible the way you have transformed your life and managed to learn so much. The way you described your home in North Carolina made me want to come visit. I think you're right, there are so many paths in life that we aren't considering and so many compelling topics we aren't introduced to. I hope I can love my life with the same openness and creativity that you do.

Sincerely,
Madison Shaffer

Dear Jacob:

The stress of school always lessens when I know a guest speaker is coming. Although you mentioned that sitting at the front of a room is not a way of educating or even speaking to a group. I personally appreciated your insights and opinions. As someone who worries about the future and college, it's nice to hear a perspective about a post-high school decision that isn't centered around expectations. I was already thinking about going on a gap year before you came, but I know now that what I want is to break away from formal education, even if for only a year.

Best of luck with your land and dreams.

Miranda Ayres

Dear Jacob:

I am thinking a lot more about how I approach my education after hearing you speak about your journey. I really felt burnt out academically and mentally after my junior year, and I want to make sure I'm ready to jump back into a classroom setting before I go to college. I am very curious, but I am not certain that that curiosity will be fulfilled within a classroom.

I want to learn more about different cultures, social justice and our relationship with the land as humans. You've inspired me to think more deeply about how I want to explore those interests out in the world next year.

Sincerely,
Lucy Brown.

PS You also inspired me to get back into foraging!

Dear Jacob:

Thank you for speaking to us about sustainable farming. The risks that industrial farming poses is very underreported. I agree too that few people know enough about the natural world they live in. If ever it collapsed tomorrow, as it could any year now, we'd have a massive famine. I am grateful that you came to our class to alert us of the crisis.

I'll be sure to e-mail you for further info. Maybe after I get my MD-PhD, I'll become a sustainable farmer myself.

Elena Lonskaya

Dear Jacob:

Your relating your life experiences opened my eyes to the different lifestyles and worlds that we can exist in if we are opened to them. It's refreshing to meet someone so passionate about the world and the way that you choose to live in it, even if that is perceived as unorthodox. I don't know if I could live the way you do, but as you said, you didn't think that you would be able to do it first either.

As someone who has struggled for happiness in life, I am so happy to see that someone akin to me has found such a joyous liberating life.

Thank you so much for coming in and talking to my class. It gave me hope for pursuit of the many things I have and want to explore over the course of my life.

I'll remind the Trader Joe's here [in Bethesda] to leave some papayas in the dumpsters for the scavengers.

Thanks again.

Nate Fellner

4

WHEN MY PEACE studies class discusses the Vietnam War, we read essays and watch a film or two. *Platoon. Coming Home.* For my students born in the late 1990s, which is all of them, Vietnam is bogged so far in the past that it comes close to being ancient history. To make it relevant, to rev the emotions, I invite Milton Brown to share his story. It is like no other the students could imagine, much less ever heard.

Born into poverty in 1950, he was eighteen and living with his grandparents in Norfolk, dreaming of becoming an accountant. With no funds for college, he was drafted into the Vietnam War. At five feet, six inches, he was the right height for combat in the miles-long network of tunnels of Cu Chi near what was then Saigon and where North Vietnamese soldiers covertly lived by day and emerged at night to battle and slay Americans. Armed with a flashlight, a bayonet, and a gun, Private Brown became a tunnel rat and a killing machine.

Today Milton can't recall how many North Vietnamese lives he took in his eleven months of tunneling—five days in and five days out—but he does remember the effect it had on his soul. "I killed so many people in the underground that only heroin helped me not to think about it," he says. "The heroin was supplied by the military, a fact not generally known by the American public. But it's true. I'm still haunted by taking the life of a boy directly in front of me. He was no older than fourteen."

Milton returned home in August 1971 a heroin addict, a blight that would last until 2008 when he nearly died by totally withdrawing in a motel room writhing in his vomit, urine, and feces. He recalls the years of addiction as "a living nightmare. I had demons. It was only God's mercy that saved me."

His two marriages failed, one from 1971 to 1978, the second from 1979 to 1982. "I was hoping my wives could help me climb out of the hole I was in. But I was too far down for them to pull me up."

Milton had two sons. One was murdered in 1997 on a Washington Street. The second refuses to talk to him. Three years ago, Milton, now clean, found night work at Wendy's and day work at a car-rental agency, both at nine dollars an hour. He now earns a bit more cleaning floors at Washington-area supermarkets on the night shift from 11 p.m. to 7 a.m., a paycheck just enough to pay rent at a small apartment in a low-income neighborhood near Union Station. He regularly sees a Veterans Affairs psychiatrist for help to deal with the traumas of Vietnam.

I met Milton five years ago when he was penniless and homeless, sleeping nights in a cardboard box on Washington's North Capitol Street across from the Government Publishing Office. For a time, he took refuge in a shelter on New York Avenue, but the noise, fighting, and being forced to leave before dawn were negatives too severe. For food, he went to the Father McKenna Center blocks from the three Senate office buildings. "What's hardest about homelessness," Milton believes, "are the vacant spaces of time, the loneliness of it all."

Milton, African American, has endured so much violence— emotional violence, military violence, street violence, racial violence, structural violence, addiction violence—that merely being alive is proof behind the often-quoted line "What matters most in life is not what we achieve but what we overcome."

In each of his many visits to the peace studies classes, Milton begins by acknowledging "my Lord and Savior Jesus Christ." One of his talks is available on YouTube. Pull up Tedx Georgetown Milton Brown.

In January 2017 Milton, at age sixty-six, enrolled in the University of the District of Columbia, taking four courses and majoring in accounting.

Dear Mr. Brown:

I retold your story to my parents last night, including every detail I could remember, and it made my mom cry. Your story is one of the few that can truly touch people, truly evoke an emotional response. I see that as an extremely important story to tell, and it is one I will never forget. The message of our class is peace, but more specifically peace through understanding. Unless we have the evidence to fully understand what war does to people, we may never form our own opinions. For me, this would have been an incomplete course without your talk. You've given everyone who heard you an inspiration that few stories could ever do. Thank you so much for taking the time out of your life to share yourself with us. We appreciate it no end.

Sincerely,
Henry Greenblatt

PS: If you ever any sort of desire to have your story on paper, I'd be happy to sit and write your memoir.

Dear Milton:

Bravery is an often-disputed topic. Typically, society promotes the idea that bravery requires physical sacrifice. That one should sweat and bleed in order to stand up for what he or she believes is just. The less-talked-about kind of bravery involves the resilience of the mind: one's ability to face their weaknesses, their strengths, their fears, and their dreams, and be able to embrace them and keep moving forward.

Mr. Brown, you have displayed both kinds of bravery. You epitomize the kind I most admire: the resilience of the mind. With the utmost candor, you relieved some of your darkest moments and exposed your soul to the class, admitted things that I would never dare say to even my closest friend. Your self-reflection and dedication to improving your life, based on introspection, shows to me that you have remarkable heart and an even more remarkable will.

Thank you for visiting our class. I'll remember your words and remember as a man who is brave, in the way that counts the most. I wish you the best of luck in continuing your studies and making progress to reconnect with your son. One day, I hope he'll see the bravery in you that I see.

Sincerely,
Elizabeth Stephens

Dear Mr. Brown:

I live with incredible privilege. While I do my best to recognize this and remind myself of it, stories like yours motivate me to use the privilege I have been granted to seek out, understand, and help those less fortunate than me. I'm not religious or spiritual myself, but your ability to identify something or someone to have so much faith in was incredibly motivational. I hope that as I get older I'll have the opportunity to meet more people like you who bear burdens greater than mine, both to recognize the extraordinary fortune I have and to understand the ways I can use it to those born with less.

Thank you for your story, your light and your positivity. I hope that one day I can become like you, believe in something as strongly as you. I hope that you may continue to find and spread the joy that you do.

Thank you,
Eliza Braverman

Dear Milton:

Yesterday you changed my life. I learned from you more than I've ever learned in school and more than I could have imagined. If I could go back and help every homeless man or woman I could have, I would. To be someone who has been on the edge and back, and to be able to inspire people the way you do, is incredible to me. More than anything, I want you to know that having people like you on this earth is a blessing, and that knowing there's always a way back gives me hope.

Stay strong, and as you have always done, never give up.

Thank you very much,
Sam Clayton

Dear Milton:

Hearing you speak yesterday was more than inspiring. You have overcome some of life's most difficult challenges. You overcame war. You over-came homelessness and you overcame addiction to one of the most dangerous drugs out there. Listening to you speak made me feel like I could overcome any challenge that comes my way. You resolve is contagious, making you a wonderful person to be around and a true inspiration. Your ability to stay strong and never give up is incredible. Continue to stay strong and stay positive. I know you will do great things.

Much love,
Brigitte Freeman

Dear Milton Brown:

I am a man of few words, and it doesn't help that your story rendered me speechless. Your experiences with overcoming addiction and homelessness is truly inspiring, and your sayings of spirituality resonated with me on a deep level.

Godspeed,
Sariya Ismail

Dear Milton:

After hearing you speak yesterday, I realized that our government is failing us. Veterans coming back from war need help that they aren't getting, and there are thousands of people living in poverty who also need help.

Your story inspired me to want to help those in my community and around the country. I don't really know what my future holds, but I know that I want to help people who are just like you. Your ability to keep going even when life really gets tough is something I hope to achieve in my life.

Your story brought me to tears. I want to thank you for sharing your knowledge about the world and our society. Just know you can always come back to our class if you need a hug.

Sincerely,
Julia Kaplan

Dear Milton Brown:

Your story has touched me. I want to thank you for being so brave and telling us about your past. I really do appreciate it. I want to thank you as well for your service in the armed forces. I hope you can conquer your demons, rather I know you can. I wish you the best of luck in regaining your son's love as well as your journey back to Vietnam.

There is a quote that goes, "Infinite love is the only truth, everything else is illusion."

I believe if you continue to do what you are doing, one day everything will come together just fine. Remember to keep loving and laughing.

Your friend,
Julian Seaton

Dear Milton:

You are the bravest man I have ever met. Thank you so much for taking the time to speak to my class about your life experiences.

Although clearly not to the same degree, I have struggled with anxiety and the thought of you facing your fears and revisiting the tunnels is admirable beyond words. Over the summer I went on a service trip with my church, and I remember how powerful songs were in binding us together and making us feel good. The way you sang was not only beautiful, but it almost moved me to tears because I could feel the passion behind yours words.

I wish you all the best and I hope you visit it again.

Lillian Wessel

Dear Mr. Brown:

Your story was truly inspiring. I have always cared about others experiencing more challenges than myself, but it can be easy to look at the world, see so many problems, and think "I can't change that." Your story inspired me to keep working to change the world, and to know that every small thing makes a difference.

I have always been lucky to have two incredible parents. I try to be appreciative of all they do for me, but yesterday I made sure to go home and say "thank you" and "I love you."

Thank you for sharing your life with us.

Sincerely,
Lucy Brown

Dear Milton:

Your story that you shared with our class yesterday struck me as one of the most inspirational messages I have ever heard. While I have been fortunate enough to live life free of many of the troubles you spoke of, I felt a personal connection to your story of finding it difficult to adjust to life after the war. My grandfather, after returning from Europe in World War II, never shared his experiences with anyone, as it was too painful to discuss.

Last year I found some of his writings, which allowed me to get an understanding of the pain he felt. For you to overcome that pain is remarkable, and I am so grateful you shared your story with us.

Sincerely,
Riley Pfaff

Dear Milton Brown:
I can't tell you how much I appreciate your coming in to talk to us. You are one of the strongest people I have ever met, and you are an inspiration. The money we gave you yesterday feels like nothing. I want to do more to help. My mom and I talked about starting a fund-raising organization to start raising funds to buy blankets and food. We would raise money until the winter and then distribute all the supplies we could buy to homeless people in DC.

There is so much we could to help, and I plan to do it. I will never again walk by a homeless person on the street without saying hi and asking how their day was. Your story has been so powerful, I think our whole class is ready to help. I hope I can meet you again.

Sincerely,
Madison Shaffer

Dear Milton:
Your story was eye-opening in a lot of ways and was really moving. I have always struggled with trying not to judge people by their first impressions, and what you said about being homeless and how people treated you spoke to me

in volumes. Every person on this planet deserves to have a good life and shouldn't be treated any differently for the circumstances that they are in.

Thank you so much for sharing your story and your wonderful singing voice. I really appreciate it, and it will stick with me for years to come.

Sincerely,
Zoe Persons

5

STEVE RISKIN, A 1975 UC Berkeley graduate, with a master's degree in Arabic Studies from Georgetown in 1981, has been a senior program officer at the United States Institute for Peace since 1994. Fluent in Hebrew and Arabic, much of his focus is the long-lasting and seemingly intractable Israeli-Palestine enmity. In 1984, President Ronald Reagan took time out from arming his favorite dictators and juntas to reluctantly sign the legislation creating the institute. At the first meeting of the board of directors, Reagan lectured the staff not to get carried away with bizarre notions like lowering the military budget or eliminating nukes: "In the real world, peace through strength must be our motto."

Not to worry. The overlords of Congress have never taken the institute seriously by backing it with real money. In 2011 it topped out at forty-three million dollars. Six years later in 2017, it sank to thirty-five million. Less than two months into office, the militaristic Donald Trump called for eliminating the institute, at the same time seeking a fifty-four-billion-dollar hike for the Pentagon, an amount that would fund the institute for 1,543 years. With one bomb-happy president after another going back to the invasion of Iraq in 1991 by sending soldiers to wage wars that couldn't be won, explained, or afforded, the institute has a noble mission backed by ignoble funding to "prevent and resolve violent international conflicts, promote post-conflict stability and development, and increase conflict-management capacity, tools and intellectual capital worldwide."

I've known many of the institute's midlevel staff and have come to admire their zeal and competence. But it must always be self-restrained, never daring to question, much less condemn, military spending or repeated interventions. Never daring to argue that instead of fighting fire with fire, wake up and fight it with water—the water of nonviolence solutions.

In June 1999, Anika Binnendjik, a star student in my B-CC peace studies class, was given five thousand dollars by the institute. In its national peace-essay contest, an annual scholarship event in which more than 2,500 high school students compete, Anika, idealistic and a lucid writer, was the Maryland state winner—a one-thousand-dollar prize—and then placed second in the nationals. Top honors went to a girl from South Dakota. All-state winners came to Washington for a week of seminars. I was one of the annual speakers, my turn coming at a breakfast for the students for the final day in Washington

After B-CC, Anika studied at Princeton, graduated cum laude, married the captain of the golf team, and earned a doctorate at Tuft's Fletcher School of Law and Diplomacy. Her dissertation, sponsored by the institute, was titled "Holding Fire: Security Force Allegiance During Nonviolent Uprisings." In 2008, Anika gave full effort on the Obama campaign and became a special assistant secretary of defense for international security affairs. With her knowledge of the mechanics and successes of nonviolence, my hope was that Anika could bring about change at the Pentagon. My larger hope was that the Pentagon never changed her.

Steve Riskin's talk to my classes blended analysis, stories, and historical allusions. His gracious manner earned unanimous affection and respect.

> Dear Mr. Riskin:
>
> Peace and nonviolent conflict-resolution tactics are perhaps our greatest weapon against violence. I love what you said about gray areas, because no conflict is black and white. There are always multiple factors at play, and I think you do an excellent job trying to investigate these and find

peaceful solutions at the root of the problem, not just scraping the surface for the short-term military intervention that creates more long-term conflict.

This is a side of government and education that we don't see as much, so thank you for taking the time to speak to us about peace and the incredible work you do.

Sincerely,
Corinne Chapman

Dear Mr. Riskin:

It felt quite ironic to hear you speak while the AIPAC policy conference was occurring [at the Verizon Center in Washington]. It was refreshing to hear a fellow Jew speak, one who is well-educated on the Israeli-Palestine conflict and not just from a pro-Israel standpoint. Your work sounds incredibly interesting, and I feel it is important. Peacemaking is crucial, yet our world often pursues it by first initiating violence. I was impressed by your knowledge of Hebrew and Arabic. I hope to one day speak both languages. Thank you for taking the time to speak to us about the relevant topic of Israel and your unique job.

Sincerely,
Lucy Brown

Dear Mr. Riskin:

I must tell you how great it is to have a fellow Bay Area native in class as a speaker. Your attitude and focus were passionate without being preachy, which can be a really hard thing to balance, I imagine, when giving a lecture. I truly wish that peace can be achieved in the world, but if it's not, I'm glad there are people like you working toward it. The US Institute of Peace is an amazing place of diversity from what I know of it. I hope that Congress recognizes as such and funds you with a budget that can afford to give Mr. McCarthy a million dollars for a Peace Studies Department at B-CC.*

Thank you for coming to class and keep making the world a better place.

Sincerely,
Nate Fellner

*Thanks, Nate, but no skimping, please. How about ten million dollars? And then how about funds for each of the twenty-six high schools in Montgomery County? After that, let's go national and get Peace Studies departments into all of the country's thirty-five thousand high schools. Check with the Congressional Budget Office for the full tab.

Dear Mr. Riskin:

I found your story—past and present—easily relatable. I am interested in the Middle East and its history from anthropological perspectives. I am intrigued by the relevance to us as a species and how it got to where it is now over the past few thousand years.

This is why I found your visit refreshing. I don't think I ever met an expert on something in which I'm so interested, despite not learning about it in school.

Thank you,
Danny Roberts

6

THE MOST FREQUENT guest speaker is Lily Flores. I invite her every semester. For me, she ranks as the most accomplished and the most life-experienced teacher at the school even though she never went past the sixth grade. Lily, in her early forties and the single mother of three, including a boy with Down syndrome, is from El Salvador. She fled her village in the mid-1980s, at the height of the civil war in which the Carter, Reagan, and Bush administrations lavishly funded and cheered on the brutal Salvadoran junta and its death squads. Some seventy-five million were killed. Largely civilians ranging from Jesuits priests to impoverished peasants. Large numbers of the government's killers were trained at Fort Benning, Georgia. No apology has ever been given by the United States to the Salvadoran victims, much less—and more important—economic reparations.

At fifteen, Lily fled. Like numberless others from that tiny country, she made her way to South Florida to labor as a field-worker picking tomatoes and cucumbers. The pay was low, tensions high. Field bosses were abusive. Living conditions were squalid, and the companies to which the crops would be sold—McDonald's and Burger King among others—were uncaring about worker's rights. Lily endured a year.

She came north, to Montgomery County, Maryland, where an older brother had settled. In time, she found work at Bethesda-Chevy Chase High School. Her job has been cleaning toilet bowls and urinals, scrubbing floors, cleaning windows, buffing walls, picking up trash in the cafeteria after breakfast and lunch.

Lily is one of the invisible at the school. Few students know her name, fewer still her background in El Salvador. Lily makes life easier for the students, cleaning up after them as they scamper by on the way to the next class.

Come talk to my students, I ask Lily. Tell them about your childhood, your days in South Florida, your children, your labors in the bathrooms. Despite a hard life, Lily has not been hardened. She sprinkles her stories with humor, as when she asks the class why is it that the girls' bathrooms are messier than the boys'. That stirs things up.

During Lily's talk one morning a few years ago, I noticed that one student, Hannah Flamm, was listening far more intently than the others. She took notes, the only one to do so. Hannah and Lily were connecting. At the end of the school day, at 2:10 p.m., students headed to the parking lots, after-school sports, club meetings, the walk home. Every student left, except one: Hannah. Where did she go? To find Lily. And she did find her—in one of the school's fourteen bathrooms. She offered to help. She did so, mop in hand that afternoon, and many more after. It was a true bonding with Lily. That summer, in 2004, Hannah went to El Salvador with a volunteer program, where she learned experientially about Lily's homeland. It would be the first of eleven visits to Hacienda Vieja, a village of some hundred families two hours by bus north of San Salvador, the capital. Her toils ranged from mentoring children to investigating the environmental and social effects of a proposed gold-mining operation.

After B-CC, Hannah went to Tufts University, majoring in political science. After earning a JD from New York University, and passing the bar, Hannah became a public interest lawyer. Classmates of Hannah had trouble understanding her befriending Lily.

I saw it as true peacemaking—a genuine reaching out to lift another person's spirit, even if it was in the smallest ways like sweeping a broom over a dirty floor.

Years later when I catch up with former peace studies students and we get to talking about our class, a common question is, "How's Lily?" She left a mark, gifted a teacher that she is.

Dear Lily:

Last year, I was completely overwhelmed by the stress of my junior year and life itself, and you caught me crying in one of the bathrooms. You comforted me and gave me tissues to dry my eyes, and waited until I had calmed down to begin cleaning. I don't know if you remember that but I do and I think about it all the time.

You were so kind to me and so patient when dealing with a hysterical sixteen-year-old.

Lily, you are so kind and inspiring. It must have been rough fleeing El Salvador so young. But you are always smiling and happy. Thank you for telling us your story.

Aliza Broder

Dear Lily:

Your story touched me in ways I can't imagine. I come from a family of immigrants from Bangladesh, and nothing hits home more than the way we find success in this land of opportunity. You have such a beautiful soul, and I want to genuinely thank you for brightening my day every time we talk in the girls' bathroom. You're my inspiration.

Much love to you and your family—

Aniqa Ahmed

Dear Lily:

When you spoke in my second period peace studies class, you expressed a desire to continue your education and get a degree. Quite frankly, I want to tell you that you have no need to, because what you know—what you have experienced—is worth so much more than any word printed in a textbook or spoken in a monotone soliloquy by a teacher. I have learned that the education system is merely a conduit of knowledge exchange that eradicates any need for students to interact with the world and gain experience.

Experience, to me, is the key to knowledge. And, Lily, you have tons and tons of it! Your courage to leave your home in El Salvador, your family, and head toward uncertainty; your works in the fields, at McDonald's. Uncertainty and your tenacious pursuit to give your children all the opportunities and security that you can muster moves me, moves me so much that I have to blink back tears in my eyes as I am writing this. You are an inspiration. If I am ever in your circumstances, I wish I can have half as much as your resolve and your sunny disposition.

Lily, Lily, Lily. You have a warm heart and gracious ways. I was touched to hear that you have never forgotten your homeland and continue to send money to your mother as well as others in your village. Your benevolence, your selfless generosity, despite your past and ongoing hardships, speak a lot about your integrity. You are a role model for people in the B-CC community who probably have more money than you and I combined. You have an advantage over them: your empathy.

In short, Lily—well not that very short—you have experienced more than all those degree wielding suits have in their entire lives. You may not be on the same pay level as them due to the ridiculous red-tape prejudice against immigrants, but you have achieved more. So be proud of that!

I am proud of you, but most importantly, I'm sure your children are too!

If you still don't believe my argument about how unnecessary education is without experience, look at a friend of mine who went to Yale University and now works in Baltimore sorting items and packing boxes for Amazon.

As you told all the girls at the end of class, Lily, "you are a flower." I'm sure you'll soon find a rich husband, especially with Mr. McCarthy leading the search for you.

Sincerely,
Elizabeth Stephens

Dear Lily:

I cannot imagine what you have been through, and more than that I cannot imagine being as giving and peaceful as you are. You, more than most, would have an excuse to be angry and bitter, but you seem hopeful and full of forgiveness. I feel that it takes a lot of strength and courage to stay soft when the world has tried to make you hard. It gives me hope that I can face adversity in my future and still have the ability to come out of it with love I my heart.

You continue to struggle with adversity yet you don't give up. I respect you for that. It must have been a monumental task to raise your children on your own in a new country. I hope you take time to support yourself, as you have gone against all odds to promote the successes of your children.

Seeing you speak brought a smile to my face and gave me hope for the world in a time filled with hatred and brutality.

I wish you the best in everything you do. Thank you so much for sharing your story with us, and helping us learn about a completely different background.

Thank you—
Dani Seltzer

Dear Lily:

I have been thinking a lot lately about how hard it is for immigrants in America, so it was great to hear your story. I spent my spring break in south Texas helping families who just came across the border from Honduras and El Salvador and were traveling to their families. They didn't know anything about schools or getting papers or going to court in front of a judge. They spoke only Spanish. It was so sad how America didn't really want to help. Thank you so much for telling your story. It inspired me to think more about how I can help all of the people leaving their countries, hoping for a better life.

Sincerely,
Lucy Brown

Dear Lily:

I am always so moved and inspired by your kindness and cheerfulness to everyone at our school. I've had days that weren't so good and your friendliness lifted up my spirits. I thank you for that. In a world full of nice people but who do cruel things, you shine like a bright star spreading kindness wherever you are.

It was gripping to hear how you immigrated to America. I know it must not have been easy. I can never imagine the fear that surrounded you in El Salvador during the civil war in the 1980s. But you were strong. I am glad you are happy where you are now.

I don't think many of us understand what happens in other countries. By sharing your story, you are educating us and inspiring change.

Thank you,
Maria Neas

Dear Lily:

You were my favorite speaker so far this year. Your stories brought tears to my eyes. You have overcome so much, worked so hard and against all odds, you are unconditionally happy and kind.

Your story of complementing a girl who was always rude to you inspired me. It reminded me to always choose kindness. Your attitude and positivity always make my day and lights up any room you are in. I am lucky to know you.

Sincerely,
Sabine Rundlet

7

F EW GUEST SPEAKERS have been as generous with their morning time than Michael Webermann. Few have come with a message that students can immediately believe in and act on. In his late twenties and a graduate of Evergreen State University, an academically progressive school in Washington, Michael is the director of FARM (Farm Animal Rights Movement), a nonprofit in Bethesda, Maryland. In middle school in Southern California, he became a vegetarian and would later go all the way to be a vegan. In other words, he has a cruelty-free diet well-grounded in personal nonviolence.

Before Michael speaks to the classes, I devote about two weeks to discuss the literature of animal rights, including the documentaries *Meat Your Meat*, *Farm to Fridge*, and *Cowspiracy: The Sustainability Secret*. Except for a small number of students who are vegetarians or vegans, the information is new. Raised in a country where the politically powerful meat, dairy, and egg lobbies see to it that killing and torturing animals for food is legal and profitable, it isn't surprising that educating students about the ethical, environmental, moral, and health arguments of peaceful coexistence with animals is taken seriously by school boards. We have physical education and sex education but no food education.

What students are rarely told in classrooms are a few facts reported in *Cowspiracy*:

- Globally, more than six million animals are killed for food every hour.

- About 82 percent of starving children live in nations where livestock animals are fed and are not starving.
- Animal agriculture is the leading cause of species extinction, ocean dead zones, water pollution, and habitat destruction.
- Animal agriculture is responsible for 18 percent of greenhouse gas emissions, more than the combined exhaust from all forms of transportation.
- Methane from livestock has a global warming power eighty-six times that of CO.
- Growing feed crops for animals consumes 56 percent of water in the United States.
- About 1.5 acres can produce 237,000 pounds of plant-based food. 1.5 acres can produce 375 pounds of meat.
- The average American eats 209 pounds of meet a year.
- One dairy cow defecates approximately 120 pounds of manure every day.

When Michael offers such information and takes questions and disagreements, he is careful to avoid being judgmental about omnivore students who eat meat and eggs and drink cow's milk. This may account for the many appreciative letters.

> Dear Michael:
>
> Mornings are a tough time. Often as not, you'll find me in first-period class, resting my head on my arm in a futile attempt to stay awake. With that in mind, I had some doubts in the beginning about the efficacy of your presentation. Some crunchy hippie was going to proselytize us for two days, before we're even awake? And while two days you certainly preached, you never preached at us. While it was still a sermon, it was extraordinarily interesting. I don't think I'll give up my steaks and hamburgers just yet, but you made me think, and for that I thank you.
>
> Michael Fine

Dear Mr. Webermann:

I really thought I would never say this, but I am preparing to go vegan one day a week. Why? Because of you, I can't thank you enough for taking two early mornings to come talk to us about something you are passionate about. Regardless of the issue, I truly respect someone like you who is actually doing something about it. This world today has too many whiners. You are certainly not one of them. You have inspired me to try vegan once a week. I can't thank you enough for that. I wish you only the best in your fight for farm animals' justice.

Respectfully,
Taylor Durban

Dear Mr. Michael Webermann:

I'm a terrible writer, so I'm really sorry if this doesn't really make sense, but thank you so much for speaking to our class about factory farms and educating us on the horrible treatment of animals. The things you said really changed me. When I went home and ate dinner, I felt terrible. I felt disgusted, and I really didn't need to feel this way. You were right. People don't need to kill animals, we don't need this. However, the only way to change things is to start with us. We can't change the industry if we can't even change ourselves. Please keep going what you are doing. I think it really helps to make people see the truth.

Nicole Colasto

PS: This is coming from a girl who ate meat last night for dinner. Thank you for really coming here.

Dear Michael Webermann:

After hearing all that you have to say, I want to become a vegetarian. Though meat is served most days in my household, I am going to try to reduce or even eliminate my consumption of it. Environmental studies is a passion of mine, and although I was aware of dead zones, I was not aware that 30 percent of the world's land is being use for agriculture/producing meat/dairy. You were extremely knowledgeable and didn't try to push any beliefs on our class. But at the same time you were very persuasive. Thank you for informing us about the harsh truth of eating meat.

Alex Taubman

Dear Michael Webermann:

I am a vegetarian and have been once since I was nine years old. Your presentation only rein-forced my reasons for making my choice. You gave me new information, enlightening me on more than I already knew. Having you come in for two days in a row was very kind of you and gave you a chance to really inform us.

Madi Hunter

Dear Mr. Webermann:

Thanks so much for coming into our class for two days. After Mr. McCarthy brought us to the issue of animal cruelty and the harmful effects that agribusiness has on our world, it didn't feel right to eat meat* But after you came, with cold statistics, extensive research, and relatable stories, I was swayed. I signed up for your e-mail and took a brochure on the way out. I am excited and hopeful to see where this takes me next.

Sincerely,
Makdes Hailu

*I've found that an effective way to get thinking about mercy to animals is with six questions:

- Do you want to reduce cruelty?
- Do you want to decrease hunger and starvation?
- Do you want to reduce global warming?
- Do you want decrease destruction to the environment?
- Do you want to decrease risks to your health?
- Do you to save money?

If the answers are yes, stop eating the flesh of animals, change from giving your money to corporations that do the killing and giving it to those who don't. Solutions to human-caused violence—inflicted globally in factory farms on millions of animals daily and on the fragilities of the planet's land, air, and water—rest with all of us and our choices.

8

RAISED ON A farm in a suburb of Detroit, Annie Mahon enrolled at the University of Michigan in 1979 to study computer science. By then, she was a veteran of the food wars. She was among the eight million sufferers of eating disorders, including anorexia, which has the highest death rate of any psychiatric illness. The majority are girls and women ages fifteen to twenty-four, according to the documentary *Dying to Be Thin*.

One of the spiritual forces that gradually freed Annie from her fears and inner confusions was a commitment to Buddhist meditation and mindfulness. She learned the arts from Nhat Hanh, the Zen master. She devoured his books and attended his retreats from Vermont to France's Plum Village. In Washington, she joined a sangha—a community of meditators—that sat every Thursday evening. She is an ordained lay Buddhist minister, licensed massage therapist, yoga teacher, and author of *Things I did When I Was Hangry: Navigating a Peaceful Relationship With Food.* "Hangry," she writes, "is when you get hungry and therefore angry. Think of it as being stressed out or angry because of one's obsessions with food and eating."

I've known Annie and her husband, Paul, since their daughter Hanna was in one of my high school classes in 2008 before going to Middlebury College and then working for a progressive labor union in New Haven. Annie and Paul fund the annual Peace Studies Awards at Bethesda-Chevy Chase High School, totaling nearly sixty thousand dollars in the first four years.

When Annie speaks to my B-CC classes, students immediately bond with her, whether because they admire her plowing through the rough patches of life or her incisive reflections about mindful cooking and eating. A line from her book is well worth remembering: "There is no way to get rid our cross, but there is a way to bear it more lightly. The first step is to recognize that we are much more than our burdens."

Dear Annie:

I cannot express how lucky I feel that you came to our class. Your message of world peace is vital for a society as anxious as ours. And your words about never finding that perfect stable place have changed my life. They made me question the idea that people have been selling me my entire life in this country: that if you do everything right, if you work 'til you drop, you'll be happy… Now that I know that this mythical place doesn't exist. I can feel free to do what I've always wanted to do in life. And I you to thank for that.

On the topic of eating disorders, I feel weird being the only person in my genetic family to have them. I never met my father, so maybe I can blame it on him. What I really blame, though, is the culture we live in for bombarding us with status symbols and not providing us with the education on how to lose weight safely. Health education fails on an epidemic level—except for Ms. Liz [the health teacher at B-CC] She's awesome.

Eating disorders are so exhausting. No one knows what it's like unless they have one. No one gets to give yourself a pep talk every time you eat or the shame around eating with other people, or being so disgusted with yourself that you can't function properly in society. It's internal warfare, and it hurts at least 99 times more than it shows. If my symptoms tell me as much, I think I've had four years in a row. From anorexia to orthrexia to binge eating to bulimia. God knows, maybe I have EDNOS now. Ha! That's terrific. Eating disorders have the highest mortality rate of any mental illness. And I believe it.

My suspicion is that therapy works very well for them though, because they depend on isolation, secrecy and a lack of self-worth. Not everyone's story is the same, not everyone wants to look the same, but it is the majority.

Hey, did I say thank you yet? Because I owe you at least that much.

I have your e-mail, so I'll keep in touch. I am no longer terrorized by school projects.

With gratitude,
Elena Lonskaya

Dear Annie:

Go Blue! It was awesome to have a Michigan grad come in to talk. It's hard to imagine what you went through but you came out on top. I was especially intrigued by your discussion on how you went through your computer science degree and how eventually found work you enjoyed doing. I'm not 100% sure what I want to study, since I only know my end goal but am reassured through your experience that I will end up doing something I enjoy. I really do encourage you to check out the alumni camp—Camp Michigania. It is on the beautiful Walloon Lake near Petoskey. You would enjoy it! Thank you so much again. Go Blue!

Katie Weber, Michigan class of 2020

9

A MONG THE CLOSEST neighbors to B-CC, none have been as generous and salient as Lakshmi Landa. Since 1996, she has been a member of the Shanti Yoga Ashram, a community of seven peacemakers with strong commitments to the works of mercy and social justice. Well more than a dozen times, I've taken my classes to the ashram to learn about meditation, anxiety reduction, and spirituality. Each commune member is employed, with the incomes pooled. Two are adjunct professors at American and George Washington universities. Lakshmi is a certified birth counselor and has had more than 350 couples enrolled in five two- to three-hour sessions to learn the techniques of breathing, relaxation, hypnobirthing, and respectful consciousness to help lower or eliminate the fears, tensions, and pains of childbirth. Before joining the ashram, of which she is codirector with her husband, Victor, Lakshmi served in the Peace Corps in the Solomon Islands after graduating from Canisius College in 1981 with a degree in accounting.

Lakshmi believes that "many, many births, up to 95 percent, could be straightforward and simple. Yet the experience is rife with interventions and is often traumatic for women and their babies. Our culture teaches women to fear birth, while we learn in hypnobirthing that one of the essentials in the birthing environment is peace. Is the mother calm and relaxed or fearful? Is the father or another companion present and supportive? Do the professional caregivers honor the family's wishes? Is there an absence of machines, people, and procedure that might interrupt the critical bonding that nature offers for the healthy emotional growth in the infant and mother?"

Lakshmi's ministry is an alternative to obstetrical violence: the high cost of conventional hospital deliveries, a pregnancy and childbirth death rate that is twice as high as Canada's, four times higher than the rate in Greece, Poland or Iceland, according to the World Health Organization. Not surprisingly, Lakshmi endorses the high-quality and low-cost work of nurse midwives and doulas. For women whose pregnancy was problem-free, she is an advocate of home births.

Before speaking to the class, the documentary *The Business of Being Born* was shown.

Dear Lakshmi:

I've been asked frequently throughout my childhood, "How many children do you want to have?" I would give the typical answer, "Oh, I don't know. Maybe one or two." I have definitely settled on a "one or none" policy now. The question was often too vast, too full of uncertainty and the unknown, for me to truly answer it with conviction. Many topics needed to be addressed before reaching a conclusion. One topic was what you came into my peace studies class to discuss the nature of childbirth.

I was a precocious—or slightly naughty child—who would wake up at 7 a.m. and plop myself in front of the television to watch TLC's *My Birth Story* series. As a result the procedures of birth were never a mystery to me. It simply seemed to be an incredibly painful process that every woman, now and again, would to endure before ending up with a healthy baby in her arm. There would be screaming, crying and cursing. And that would be that.

I thought I understood childbirth when I was young. Of course, I was wrong.

As you said during your discussion, birth is sacred. I came to realize that in in my own time. It is a raw process, exposing the fundamental nature of human kind, that enlightened everyone involved in the preciousness of life. Unfortunately, childbirth, especially the natural kind, has been stigmatized and distorted. Many women fear it. Your explanation on the cyclical relationship of fear, stress, and tension show how potent this stigma remains, as well as how the much of the medical industry preys on the ignorance and fears of women and men.

Thank you for opening my eyes to the options of natural childbirth. To me, that now seems like the more sensible option over C-sections and drug assisted birth.

Thank you for reminding me how precious life is.

Sincerely,
Elizabeth Stephens

Dear Lakshmi:

Thank you for taking time out of your day to speak to my class. Our new topic of childbirth has been compelling and has shed light on issues I was not aware of. I have always thought of hospitals as safe places, but I didn't realize women could be so manipulated and mistreated during childbirth by doctors. I have come to appreciate home births and midwives, especially after hearing you speak yesterday. When I have children, I will definitely consider having a midwife / home birth. Thank you for all your devotion and hard work toward peace in every way.

Brigitte Freeman

Dear Sister Lakshmi:

I really appreciate your coming to talk to our class. Before a couple days ago I had never really thought about birth. Mr. McCarthy says that there are two things in life that only happen once: birth and death. As a society we focus heavily on death but not so much birth.

I always just assumed I would give birth in a hospital, but now I'm considering doing more research on midwives. If the baby is really conscious and can be affected by the birth experience, then why not have the most peaceful birth possible? The ideas you presented us with were mind opening. You are totally right when you say that being pregnant is not an illness. I will start sharing these ideas with my friends and family, in hopes of sparking their curiosity. I think if everyone took a second to think about it, we would all chose to have natural births.

Sincerely,
Madison Shaffer

Dear Lakshmi:

Before you came to our class, I had never thought much about birth and the pain, violence, and business tied to it. You made a compelling and rational case for avoidance of hospitals for childbirth. They are generally unnecessary. They practice violence, they damage the baby's psyches, and they cause mothers great suffering. After all,

95 percent of births are issue-free. Going to the hospital is fine when something goes wrong, but in the vast majority of births much of what many obstetricians do is stress the mothers—making it hard to relax and easy to feel more pain.

The link of business to hospital births was the most fascinating part for me. So many things that we take for granted are part of our culture—from engagement rings to mouthwash to hospital childbirths—are not needed and were actually implanted by corporate interests. That money controls something so personal and sacred as birth is a testimony to the power of big business in America and speaks to our need to stand up and fight back against these powers.

Thank you so much for coming to our class and help open my mind a little more.

Sincerely,
Conor Smythe

Dear Lakshmi:

At the beginning before you started talking I assumed that most of the stuff you had to say was mumbo-jumbo crap. But I was wrong. You made some excellent points about how high-stress environments wouldn't exactly make it easy for mothers and babies.

I'm still skeptical but thank you from the nonbelievers like me.

Tom Pahl

Dear Lakshmi

It was fascinating to learn about hypno-birthing. I loved hearing about your experiences and knowledge of how giving birth as changed over thousands of years and that for a long time it was mostly pain-free. I think it's really important for women and families to understand that having a baby should not be stressful. We need more people like you to share your perspective so women do not have to be in fear about a natural process that brings life into the world.

It as really eye-opening and changed my opinion on hospital births. I also really enjoyed the books you brought in. I plan to read them soon.

Thank you—
Elizabeth Mulvihill

Dear Lakshmi:

As an aspiring doctor and possibly a future midwife, I cannot tell you how intrigued I was by your stories about childbirth. Your thoughts and knowledge engaged me for all forty-five minutes of our class. As someone who is easily distracted, that is quite an accomplishment. Quite honestly, your commentary on the mind of body of women and their children made me ever more excited to become a mother. However, I should probably hold off saying that to save my dad from a heart attack.

The importance of the mother-child bond is incredible and your belief on the need to decrease fear when giving birth is something I will always remember.

All the best—
Sarah Payne

Dear Lakshmi:

Thank you so much for coming to speak to our class yesterday. It was interesting to learn about alternatives to childbirth because the conventional way has always sounded scary to me. My mom didn't use any drugs when she had my siblings and me, and I always thought she was crazy for that. Now I am thankful for it, because she said that all of us were very alert and calm after our births. Not that I plan on having children anytime soon but this will definitely stick with me if that time ever comes. Thank you again for speaking to us.

Sincerely,
Zoe Persons

10

F ROM B-CC, IT'S a mile south to 6701 Wisconsin Avenue and
the Oneness Family School, which Andrew Kutt founded in
1988. With a modest grub stake of fifty thousand dollars in bor-
rowed money, he began with seven children in a spare room in a local
library. His educational commitment was to the beliefs and teaching methods of Maria Montessori, the Italian physician who opened
an elementary school in the slums of Rome in 1907. A specialist
in peace education and conflict resolution, he understands that it is
never too early for children to learn that alternatives to violence exist.
Two-year-olds are as welcome as ten-year-olds.

Andrew Kutt is a graduate of Assumption College in Worcester,
Massachusetts, which is the hometown of Jim McGovern, one of the
most progressive members of Congress. After Assumption, he did
graduate work at the University of Tubingen in Germany and the
University of North Carolina, on the way to earning his Montessori
master teaching certification at the Institute for Advanced Studies in
Maryland.

When speaking to my classes about the grit he needed to open
a school—finding a building, hiring teachers, recruiting students—
Andrew comes with his acoustic guitar. He is a singer and songwriter,
at ease with "Blowin' in the Wind" as he is with his own songs.

> Dear Andrew:
> I don't know the last time I heard an
> inspirational talk that rang as true as yours did

that featured guitar playing. Your rendition of "Blowin' in the Wind" and your own songs were both brilliant and pleasantly emotionally stirring and calming. Your optimism and immense focus on the growth and love of people felt extremely refreshing and authentic. It's hard to see the good in things when obstacles are constantly being thrown at you, yet you are unwavering in your strong will and passion to open your school no matter what happened. Your commitment to enjoying life through learning is infectious and reminded me why I've always loved the notion of teaching. Thank you for reminding kids that they are special and the world is their playground to live life. I just hope you remember how special you are through your work and your ideals. I appreciate your coming to class, and please, for the sake of humanity, keep up the good work.

Sincerely,
Nate Fellner

Dear Andrew:

I thought it was brave of you to sing something so heartfelt in a classroom of teenagers. I love the concept of your school. Democratic learning, I hope, is the education of the future. We can only hope that your school expands and the concept catches like wildfire (whisper of a dream)! Thank you for sharing your story with the class. I'll keep it in mind when we discuss educational philosophy. What do you think of John Taylor Cratto?

Sincerely,
Elena Lonskaya

Dear Mr. Kutt:

I know the feeling of not knowing what you want to do with yourself but perhaps not as well as you have known it. I am thrilled to see that you took your passion and have been so successful with it. They say that if you like what you do for work every day, then it's not really a job. I hope I can experience this someday, just as you do now. Thank you for coming to our class. Maybe we can have a guitar jam session. Sometime. Until then, I wish you happiness and even more success.

Sincerely,
Katie Vicenzi

Dear Andrew:

My mother is a principal, and I can imagine how much goes into coming up with ideas for your school and how to run it in an effective a way. I had a friend, Ellen, who went to Oneness Family School and absolutely loved it. Not many people can say that they liked middle school, but the people who went to Oneness can because of you. Thank you also for sharing your wonderful songs and singing voice with us. You are extremely talented. I hope your expansion of Oneness to a high school goes well, and I wish you all the best in your future endeavors.

Mallory Mical

11

NOT MANY SPEAKERS come to the classes in their work clothes. An exception was Dr. Matthew Picard, a board-certified physician in pediatrics and in neonatal perinatal medicine. In green scrubs, he shared stories of his twenty years of trying to save the lives of babies born prematurely at Holy Cross Hospital in Silver Spring, Maryland. Some deliveries were uncomplicated, vaginal, and inducement- and epidural-free, others were unpredictable and C-sectioned. Dr. Picard, a history major at Harvard in the mid-1980s and a 1990 graduate of Stanford University School of Medicine, spoke of the emotional pressure of making life and death decisions—the elation of defying the bleak odds by saving a baby weighing less than two pounds and the anguish of seeing a life fade away.

Dr. Picard, a marathon runner who married a Harvard classmate, is the father of Sonia, a B-CC senior and one of the more engaged students in the peace studies class.

> Dear Dr. Picard:
> You probably have the most honorable job in the world. You save the lives of the tiniest babies there are. That's pretty incredible. I was a premature baby and was in NNICU for some time. It's nice to know that you have people looking out for you in your earliest days and even

before you're born. Thank you so much for doing what you do. Keep saving those lives.

Best,
Eva Chesivoir

Dear Dr. Picard:

I never knew the heart-pounding action that neonatologists like yourself experience every day. That you save the lives of new life day in and day out astounds me. Not only are you able to contribute so significantly to saving people, but you also manage to balance a schedule that allows you to be a family man. That amazes me, and I applaud your commitment to both your professional life and your personal life.

I couldn't imagine the tragedy and stress you must feel on a regular basis working in your medical field, but as those Christmas parties and reunions serve to remind you, it really may be worth it to give so many babies a chance at having a life. Thank you for coming to our class, and keep being an everyday hero of humanity the way now have been for decades. Just don't be afraid to retire someday. You'll have earned it.

Sincerely,
Nate Fellner

Dear Dr. Picard:

Earlier this semester, we had a woman come in and talk about hypnobirthing. So when you came, it was nice to hear your side of things. Not many people can say that they save lives—but you can, and I think that is amazing. Your stories were truly inspiring and I'm sure hundreds if not thousands of families are grateful to you. Thank you so much for talking to us about what causes premature births and the importance of prenatal care. We aren't taught those things in school, so it was really interesting to learn, especially since some of us as parents will be going through that at some point in our lives.

Thanks again for coming in,
Mallory Mical

Dear Dr. Picard:

Every year for career day at North Chevy Chase Elementary when we had to rate from one to five on the careers we wanted to go to (one being the least interested), you were always at the top four or five. It was funny listening to the difference the way you spoke to us in elementary school and now. Kinda bummed you didn't bring any props for us to take home.

I was actually born at Holy Cross hospital, and I think it is so cool that you work there. Your job is very important to society, and I can only imagine the number of babies lives you have saved.

It also was calming to hear that you studied history in college and then went to medical school because it is freaking me out with college around the corner and what I want to do with my life. Thank you so much for coming to visit with us. You'll probably hear from Sonia soon that she's with me.

Thanks,
Cindy Pontachack

12

ONE OCTOBER 5, 2012, Michael Sullivan, a serious-minded member of my first-period peace studies class wrote a good-faith letter attempting to illuminate me about the benefits of football. More than once in class I had argued that football, a violent, unhealthy, and high-risk game should be dropped and the football field be turned into a garden, first, to raise crops for Washington's homeless shelters and, second, to be the scene of an elective course in urban agriculture.

"Without football," Michael wrote, "I would not be the person I am today. I would be a little undisciplined punk. That's what football does; it teaches you discipline and the most basic forms of it. It teaches you how to overcome adversity when times get rough. It teaches you teamwork and how to get along with people of different races, religions, and interests to achieve the mutual goal of success. It teaches you accountability. Responsibility. Determination. It teaches you how to work hard. Overall, football prepares for life. Honestly, football builds character and makes our lives more stable. Yes, it is violent. Yes, one could argue that it's sexist or that females can't keep up with the physical demands. But my intentions are good."

Never to be doubted. My admiration for Michael increased for his taking the time and making the effort to thoughtfully explain his opinions. Nothing he said were garbage arguments, of the kind Daniel Snyder makes when he refuses to drop the name Redskins—the Washington team he owns.

In January 2017, Michael, then in his final semester Towson University near Baltimore, spoke to the classes about the perils of college drinking. The annual number of fatalities from alcohol poisoning or alcohol abuse is imprecise, but it is safe to say that more than a few mothers and fathers will receive a phone call from a college saying their child is dead, what funeral arrangements would you prefer. It's also true that the last words of parents as they send their child off to college is "have a lot of fun getting drunk."

Michael spoke forcefully about his opposition to college drinking. He took time also to describe the ten-day service trip he took with his Towson classmates. After graduation, Michael joined AmeriCorps. No surprise there.

Dear Michael:

As a high school senior, I am familiar with the party and drinking culture. I have seen numerous people sent to hospitals. I have had to keep people awake. It really is a huge problem for my generation. Especially with new flavored drinks, it is easy for us to drink too much. I also think there is a huge problem with the culture that praises people who can drink excessively. It leads to binge drinking and dangerous intoxication levels.

Your stance is a rare one for a college student, so I enjoyed hearing that perspective from someone like you and not a teacher or a parent. I think it made the message more real.

I also liked hearing about your work in the Dominican Republic and Puerto Rico. I am thinking of a gap year and what you said really excited me instead of the nervousness I was feeling. I am proud to know you are a B-CC graduate. Thank you for coming back and sharing your stories.

Dani Seltzer

Dear Michael:

College is on all of our minds, so hearing about it is always informative. We always hear about all the good parts of college, but hearing about the drinking and all the bad things because of alcohol was something we needed to hear.

I'm glad also that you showed us the good things in college, the helping people by building houses and exploring other countries.

Thank you coming to our class.

Sincerely,
Alexa Gonzalez

Dear Mike:

As I apply and prepare for college, I need all the advice I can get. Hearing what Mr. McCarthy said when introducing you about the ABCs of college (Abusing, Boozing, and Cruising) was helpful.

In addition, I was especially interested in your experience abroad. Although it was short, your service trip to the Dominican Republic sounded like a lot of fun and clearly had a powerful impact on both the people you met and helped there.

Good luck in whatever you may pursue in the future.

Sincerely,
Conor Smythe

Dear Michael:

I have to say that I wish you were the one giving assemblies to students about drug and alcohol safety. Your understanding but careful advice could really help people to feel their limits and not be consumed by alcoholism as well as preventing possible sexual assaults from occurring. I absolutely believe in the "don't drink from a stranger's cup" mantra. Your life philosophy of mindfulness is refreshing, and I wish more people, including myself, would stop and just take in the world once in a while. Maybe we would all feel a little bit more sensible. Thank you for coming in and please keep being as mindful as you have been, so that we can all be a little better off.

Sincerely,
Nate Fellner

13

T INKERING AND DABBLING in his kitchen after returning to his Bethesda home in 1998 after a morning run, Seth Goldman was mixing a scattering of ingredients in a thermos to come up with a drinkable beverage that was high in organics and not sugary. That was nearly twenty years ago when Goldman, less than a decade from earning a graduate degree from Yale, gave little thought that what was happening in his kitchen, with his wife Julie looking on, would soon become Honest Tea, a marketable beverage that is now on the shelves of more than one hundred thousand stores from mass-sales supermarkets to neighborhood independents. In 2015, sales totaled three hundred million bottles.

"The first ten years were really lean and challenging," Seth told the peace studies classes about the partnership he formed with Barry Nalebuff, one his graduate school professors. Dealing with distributers, bottlers, organic sugar farmers in Paraguay and dominant corporations had to be done on the run, amid stumbles and high and low hurdles: "We were breaking even, so we weren't losing a ton of money. We had to get investors to raise money to help us grow. And if we succeed, you'll get your money back. Our founding investors, those who wrote us checks in 1998, ten years later they earned twenty-six times their money. They took a risk and were rewarded."

As was Seth Goldman. What began as a long-shot company looking for a modest market share was sold in 2008 to Coca-Cola, a deal that earned the former tinkerer and dabbler "tens of millions of dollars," according to *The Washington Post*. Despite the muscular distribution powers of Coke—the world's largest soft drink company—competition for consumer dollars remains fierce. Aside from shelves stacked with "sports drinks" from Gatorade to Powerade, are those holding the competitors of Honest Tea: Lipton's Diet Green Tea, Snapple's Raspberry Tea, Pure Leaf Lemon Tea, Gold Peak Tea, and Organic Black Tea, among others.

Seth Goldman, a vegetarian committed to animal rights, a bicycle commuter, and someone who drinks no alcohol, is a B-CC parent. Born in 1965 and raised in Wellesley, Massachusetts, he majored in politics and government at Harvard. Adventuresome, he traveled to China and Russia to teach English after graduation. Returning home at twenty-three, he signed on as a campaign worker when Michael Dukakis ran for the presidency with his running mate Lloyd Bentsen. They lost to George H. W. Bush and Dan Quayle who in 1992 would be defeated by Bill Clinton and Al Gore.

Freed from the daily operations of Honest Tea, he has aligned himself with Beyond Meat, a California plant-based start-up aiming to break into the health food market with an alternative to animal flesh. "I'm fired up every day about I'm doing," he said, placing himself among those who see Beyond Meat as saving animal lives, decreasing global warming, protecting the environment, and taking on the vast negative power of animal agriculture. "With Beyond Meat, we have a chance to transform not just diets but what happens to our ecosystem or to animals. But I have to keep in mind, even if I care passionately about protecting the lives of all creatures, I have to make sure this product is competitive. Most people will buy Beyond Meat only if it tastes delicious, if it works well on a grill, if it goes well with ketchup and mustard. We have to be commercially competitive."

With a few minutes remaining before still one more bell called the students to the exit ramps, but not before leaving behind more than seventy bottles of Honest Tea to slake a few thirsts, Seth Goldman summed up his personal philosophy: "There is an easy formula for happiness. It's when what you have is greater than what you want. Most people would say the way to be happy is to have more. I say the way to be happy is to want less."

Dear Seth:

Even before you came to our class, Honest Tea was one of my favorite beverages. Besides its incredible taste, your company's commitment to Fair Trade and transparency in its business dealings is so admirable in this age where large companies can get away with almost anything. Your dedication to your consumers, and determination to not compromise your values, is something we can all learn from and apply to anything in our lives.

Honest Tea forces me to consider the repercussions of my purchases, and I will be sure to look more closely at the food and other products I buy in hopes that they are all made honestly!

Thank you for speaking and for the delicious tea you gave us. I hope one day I'll be able to make something as far reaching and enjoyable as you.

Sincerely,
Cate Paterson

Dear Mr. Goldman:

Although your entrepreneurial prowess is admirable, Mr. McCarthy said best what is your most inspiring trait: unlike the majority of the population that is idealistic (myself included), you have dedicated yourself to applying your ideas to reality and fulfilling yourself mentally, ethically, spiritually, and physically. That kind of commitment requires a selfless and tenacious heart, which I and (I'm sure) my classmates appreciate.

Seeing your lifestyle, your travels, your environmental awareness, and perception of social struggles and the fruits of your labor, Honest Tea, Beyond Meat, and your happiness, I am motivated to become a more active local and global citizen. Like you, I wish to advocate for a healthier food culture and eating habits. However, I think I will remain behind the scenes as a biological chemist or food scientist rather than a company owner. I'm not extroverted enough for that!

Your efforts in promoting a vegan or vegetarian lifestyle not only demonstrate your compassion for animals, the environment and humans, but it also reveals your enlightened perception of the world. You have momentarily (for a couple hours!) swayed me to become a vegetarian. But alas, I don't have enough self-control to do that yet. Although I don't eat pork or beef anymore, I'm still addicted to egg-salad sandwiches!

One day, I'll have the guts to apply my ideals to my life and transition from a mentality of unconscious cruelty to conscious compassion.

Thank you for sharing your experiences and sharing your smile!

Sincerely,
Elizabeth Stevens

Dear Mr. Goldman:

It makes me hopeful to see the intersection of ethics and the environment with businesses and profits. America generally prides itself on its capitalist system and I really do think people vote with their wallets. As a candidate, or product, it is not enough to simply be okay, you have to be amazing and I think that is what you are striving for: making it easier for people to align their ethics with their actions.

As a longtime vegetarian trying to take it to the next level and become a vegan, I am sometimes horrified at my lapses. How is it that I can put cream cheese on my bagel when I wouldn't be able to abuse a cow? I hope companies like yours will reach beyond that 5 percent of the public who are vegetarians and provide some future assurance that things will only get better, that the curve of the of our choices is going up.

Sincerely,
Mian Osumi

Dear Mr. Goldman:

Hearing your joy for Honest Tea and Beyond Meat was infectious and inspiring. It's incredible how far both companies have come (with good reason!) and with everything the companies stand for. By having Beyond Meat widely available to the public, you are changing not only diets but also the standards of quality ingredients and production.

I have been a vegetarian for almost a decade now, and I often find is difficult to not only find vegetarian food that I like but that my family could enjoy too. Beyond Meat is a staple in our household and at least for my family, is changing how we eat all together.

Sincerely,
Olivia Mozdzierz

Dear Mr. Goldman:

The food industry and our disconnect from where our food is coming from has disturbed me for a while. Even more so, I'm passionate about

decreasing the environmental and economic burdens that the food industry inflicts. It was inspiring to see someone with similar passions go out
and make something of them in a way that is
accessible and widespread. It was clear that you
love what you do, and honestly, as I face adulthood and the pressures of choosing what to do
with my life, it was very reassuring.

Your point about the difference between
knowledge and wisdom also struck a chord
with me. I really want to get out and experience
as much as I can, and learn from being out in
the world because this education is equally if
not more important than what we learn in the
classroom.

Thanks for sharing your story with us.

Sincerely,
Isabel Brown

PS: I'm in the process of going vegan and I love
the Beyond Meat products.

Dear Mr. Goldman:

Your talk to our class this week was extremely
meaningful for me, not just because of the issues
you are trying to resolve but because of the methods you are using. We've spoken a lot about activism this year in peace studies, but we have not
discussed the ability of companies and business-
men to create meaningful change through innovation and invention. I was also grateful to hear
about your fair-trade agreements with farmers
in Paraguay. I actually went on a service trip to
rural Paraguay in 2014 and lived with a family
that participated in a similar agreement (maybe

with Honest Tea!). It really did make a difference in their lives. Thank you for doing what you do, and thank you for speaking to our class.

Sincerely,
Riley Pfaff

Dear Mr. Goldman:

Your story really spoke to me personally, because you started from nothing and made a huge, very successful company. I am going to Savannah College of Art and Design this fall and hope to either be a graphic designer or fashion designer. And I want to be successful in one of those fields. When I hear stories like yours, it inspires me to work harder to fulfill my dreams and goals. Keep making amazing drinks. Thank you so much!

Sincerely,
Sonia Picard

14

F OR MORE THAN two decades, Ann Brown has been consulting with nonprofits ranging from Friends of the Earth to Clean Water Action to the Coalition of Immokalee Farmworkers. While a student at Carleton College in Minnesota in the early 1980s, one of her political science professors was Paul Wellstone. Ever urging and advising his students to get involved in electoral politics, it eventually happened that he followed his own counsel—starting by running for local offices and winning a US Senate seat in 1990. On the far left, he was Bernie before Bernie. He was one of only eleven senators who voted in 1991 and 2002 against resolutions to invade Iraq. Campaigning for a third term, he was killed in a snowstorm plane crash with his wife and daughter eleven days before the 1996 election. His political philosophy sprang from his view to "never separate the life you lead from the words you speak."

That can be said of Ann Brown. Much of her talk to the class, which included her daughter Lucy who had been accepted at Oberlin, focused on her consulting with the Alliance to End Slavery and Trafficking (ATEST).

> Dear Ms. Brown:
>
> I've been a friend of Lucy's since the fourth grade, but I had no clue her mom was so great. Slavery is alive and well here in Montgomery County, and it's people like you, modern aboli-

tionists, who fight for our soul as a community and as a people. Keep up the good fight, please.

Thank you,
Danny Roberts

Dear Ann Brown:

I never knew that trafficking was such a major problem in this world until I had a chance to listen to you speak. Hearing you discuss how trafficking has affected our world today and the amount of trafficking crimes that have been reported in our area was inspiring. I hope to one day become like you and speak out to our community and let them know that trafficking is something that will stay around if something is not done about it.

Sincerely,
Tyjhan

Dear Mrs. Brown:

I am one of the students from AP world who attended your talk in peace studies this past Friday. I was the girl asking a lot of questions. Thank you so much for coming to our school to talk, because as you said, it is important to talk about these issues. I found your experiences both riveting and inspirational, and I hope to one day work with similar organizations in the field of human rights law.

Thanks again,
Liza Brilliant

15

ON AUGUST 3, 2016, a presidential record was set: Barack Obama granted clemency to 214 federal inmates, the largest single-day release ever. It brought to 562 clemencies, a number higher than ones issued by the previous nine presidents combined. Sixty-seven of those Obama freed were lifers. Nearly all the men and women had been convicted of nonviolent drug crimes, going back to the Reagan era when rabids like William Bennett—the self-promoting drug czar—led the lock-'em-up-for-life movement.

Among those heartened by the releases was Jessica Cobbett, a former peace studies student and B-CC class of '09. She is on the staff of Mission Launch, a Washington and Baltimore-based non-profit whose work is reducing recidivism and helping to eliminate the bias against released federal and state prisoners. The United States ranks as the world's most punitive nation, having less than 5 percent of the planet's population but 25 percent of its prisoners. More then 650,000 people are annually released from minimum security, medium security, maximum and supermax security prisons—with as many as 60 percent returning. Mission Launch, which recently won a $1.2 million grant from the Open Society Foundation, is directed by Teresa Hodge and Laurin Hodge, a mother-daughter team. Teresa Hodge survived a seventy-month sentence on a white-collar, nonviolent, first-time offense. Up close, she saw the dark realities of both prison life and the negativities that former inmates can face when looking for work or social acceptance.

"Wouldn't it make sense to invest in the education systems in the United States and less on locking up people?" Jessica asks. "I am not alone in asking this question, yet most people will try to refute this by asking the classic question, 'but what about the murderers and rapists?' But who are the people behind bars? As children, we're made to believe that the prison system is great because it keeps everyone safe from all the horrible people who seemingly cannot be a healthy part of society. This is not the case. Almost half the prison population is serving time for nonviolent offenses like drug-related offenses or petty theft. One of my roles with Mission Launch is to confront such misconceptions and stigmas while working to increase empathy and understanding. Far too often, people turn a blind eye to the prison system by assuming that everyone doing time brought it on themselves, discounting statistics highlighting the severity of institutional racism poverty."

Jessica grew up in South Africa during the final years of Apartheid in the 1990s. "Political conversations and opinions took place all around me nonstop," she recalls. "It was not until I was older and began reading about Mandela that I was hastily pulled out of my bubble and confronted with the reality that he had been imprisoned for decades for fighting for equality, justice, and peace. It was about then that I started to feel skeptical about prisons and any type of system that punished people, questioning their validity and effectiveness."

After her years at B-CC, Jessica earned a degree in Ethnicity and Multiculturalism at the University of Bristol, England. "I decided to return to the United States to get involved in challenging one of the largest human rights violations facing the country today—mass incarceration... One of the most heartbreaking cases I have encountered is of a man who was sentenced to ten years for a crime he did not commit. He pleaded guilty because he was told that he would not win the case at court and if he did not plead guilty he would get twenty years. How is this justice? He now spends his days running his own nonprofit that supports children while their parents are incarcerated. He knows too well the pain of separation during prison and does what he can to affect positive change."

In 2015, Rep. Bobby Scott, a Virginia Democrat, and Rep. Jim Sensenbrenner, a Wisconsin Republican, introduced the Safe, Accountable, Fair, and Effective Justice Act.

The legislation proposes needed reforms in sentencing, parole, rehabilitation, and prosecution. Despite wide bipartisan support, the bill has yet to come to the House floor for a vote—which increases the need for more advocates like Jessica Cobbett.

Dear Jessica:

Your visit to our class struck a chord within me. I left the class feeling frustrated due to the realization that we have such a long way to go before people understand the difference between what is just and what is morally unjust. Yet I also left with a feeling of hope and gratitude because if there are more people like you out there, who come to schools and bring up topics never seen in our curriculum, then maybe we have a chance. A chance for students to learn the severity of these issues, break free from our four-walled class-rooms, and solve the real problems of society, not just math problems.

I wish you good luck in your battle for reform. Hopefully, I will see you again in this fight.

Thank you,
Liza Brilliant

Dear Jessica:

Your talk made a compelling case for prison reform. I was already convinced of the need for change before you came in, and your talk has further cemented that belief in my mind. The statistics you shared, like how the US has 5 percent of the world's population but 25 percent of the world's population, how one in eleven white males will go to prison compared to one in thre blacks males, how the majority of prisoners are nonviolent offenders and how ex-inmates get trapped in a vicious, cruel, and racist criminal justice system, serves to illustrate the unfairness, cruelty, and racism of it all.

Personally I believe that we must transition from a punishment to a rehabilitation focused system.

Thank you for taking the time to talk with us. I hope to join you in the future in fighting for reform of our corrupt, cash-controlled criminal justice system.

Thank you,
Conor Smyth

PS: I think your most credible point was the loophole for modern slavery in our prisons. It's amazing I have heard so little about this because it surely one of the most horrifying aspects of American society.

Dear Jessica:

I gotta say, you made prison come across even worse than I'd already imagined. As the son of a defense attorney, I have grown up to dislike institutions akin to prisons and inherently knew of many of the general injustices that occurred in prison. However, your specificity in talking to us allowed me to be freshly horrified and outraged. The racism reflected in the proportion of black to white prisoners in DC is disgusting. It cannot be easy to fight for the rights of people that society wants to discard as "amoral" or "bad," but they are still human beings and they still have rights. Thank you for reminding me of this and showing us the merit of your fights in your talk to our class.

Sincerely,
Nate Fellner

Dear Jessica:

Thank you for opening up our class to a discussion otherwise ignored in American education. Your talk, as well as your leadership, introduced thoughts and ideas I hadn't pondered before and revealed new things about the beliefs of myself and my classmates.

In my personal opinion, it is without question that we need reform in our prison systems, abolition of the death penalty, and better investigations into the disparities of the incarceration rates in America. That it is not a topic of great debate within my school, let alone the country as a whole, comes as no great surprise and sparks my interest even further into the criminal justice system and the rights of those who have fallen victim to it.

I have great admiration for the effect you have had on my class and our school in a mere forty-five minutes.

Sincerely,
Sydney Jesus-Allen

Dear Jessica:

Your talk yesterday was incredibly thought-provoking. I left the room feeling more knowledgeable about the prison system, as well as more compassionate and empathetic to the struggles that former prisoners face. While I don't have any personal connections to anyone in prison, it as heartwarming to know there are people like you looking out for them.

I found your words especially moving because you asked for insights from students which allowed me to see some of the different perspectives on the subject. I was surprised that prisons actually use prisoners for free labor. That is something I had only seen in *Orange Is the New Black*.

Thank you for everything you do and for speaking to our class.

Sincerely,
Sarah Mayhew

16

E BULLIENT, WITTY, AND with unrestrained self-confidence, Zane Chesivoir rarely failed to regale my class. Sometimes it was his reaction to an essay on Gandhi; other times it might be making a counterargument to one of his classmate's opinion. After B-CC he took his talents to Guilford College, a Quaker haven in North Carolina. From the evidence, one of the talents includes stand-up comedy, laced into his talk to the classes on his last visit to B-CC.

Dear Zane:

Your impersonations of different characters and people were hysterical! I hope one day you achieve your goal of doing comedy and I guarantee I will be at one of your shows. The struggles you shared about college were eye-opening and made me realize that college isn't all about fun. I wish we had more time in class for you, but I am honored I had the opportunity to meet you.

Grace Rosen

Dear Zane:

I loved your impersonations! It was so great to meet someone who is so excited about school, specifically peace studies. Your advice about college was very helpful and informative. I know now that there may be rough patches throughout college, but I shouldn't drop out or give up when things get hard. I wish you the best, and I hope you see many more amazing synthetic theater shows.

Sincerely,
Jenna Troccoli

Dear Zane:

Your vibrancy for life gave me hope for the future. At this point in the school year, it's easy to think all hope is lost and to adopt a life of doom and gloom. Your refusal to have given into that, as well as your example of your own brand of mindfulness, allowed me to believe that it does get better. Keep performing and never let anyone take away your imagination because you are extraordinary.

Thanks,
Danny Roberts

Dear Zane:

I'm usually exhausted first thing in the morning, though your visit woke me right up. Few people bring that amount of energy into a classroom, and it really helped invigorate me for the rest of the day. In addition to that you helped give me a sense of what to expect from college, and for a second semester senior no information is more valuable than that.

Thank you so much for taking the time to visit our class.

Best wishes,
Nate R.

17

AFTER ONLY A few minutes of speaking to the class, it was blindingly obvious that Chuck Booker, pastor of the Bethesda Presbyterian Church since 2009, was a living example of the adage that it isn't what you achieve in life, it's what you overcome. When in his early twenties—he is now fifty-five—he struggled to withstand the pains of alcoholism and depression. He endured three hospitalizations before making what has been called his "night-into-light journey." With the help of Alcoholics Anonymous, he stopped drinking in 1994.

Of his comeback, Reverend Booker wrote in his essay "From the Brokenness of Addiction to the Healing of Communion": "First, let us confess that each of us is caught in addictive cycles, and that we are powerless to change them as individuals. Based on our fear of scarcity, we are caught in lifestyles of consumerism and entitlement that find expression in an all-too-human desire to possess rather than steward, to abuse rather than enjoy, to numb through excitement rather than delight through awareness. Each of us is driven to exploit external sources of God's created pleasures in an attempt to palliate internal sources of fear."

Before accepting a pastorate at the Northside Presbyterian Church in Ann Arbor, Michigan where he would serve for eleven years, Reverend Booker worked in Tucson, Arizona, in 1991 with Central American refugees fleeing death squads, torturers, and chaos in their homelands. What he learned would lead him years later to be stashed for three months in a federal prison in Bradford, Pennsylvania, that held three hundred inmates serving stretches mostly for drug use. In 2001, two months after 9/11, he was arrested along with thirty-six others for the misdemeanor of trespassing at Fort Benning, Georgia. The nation's largest military base was home to the School of the Americas, better known as the School of Assassins where recruits from Latin American juntas were taught to be killers. Every third week in November thousands of human rights activist have demonstrated for twenty-seven years at the gate of the base. Crossing the line can mean a six-month sentence and a five-thousand-dollar fine. The director of the annual SOA event is Roy Bourgeois, a Vietnam veteran and a former Maryknoll Catholic priest who was stripped of his sacerdotal privileges by the Vatican of Pope Francis for advocating the ordination of women to the priesthood.

For Chuck Booker, the SOA was "a school of terrorism on our own soil." The murderers of Archbishop Oscar Romero on the morning of March 24, 1980, during mass were graduates of SOA. Months later three Catholic sisters and a laywoman were slain by SOA alumni. Salvadoran death squads trained at Fort Benning were rampant during the 1980s of that country's blood-drenched civil war, including the massacre of nine hundred men, women, and children in the village of El Mozote as well as the slaughter of six Jesuit priests.

Not long before his assassination, Archbishop Romero pleaded with President Jimmy Carter to cease sending military aid to the Salvadoran government. The aid that is needed, crucially so, is food, clothing, medicine: anything but weapons. Carter ignored Romero's request. At the time of his killing, the prelate was the eleventh Catholic priest slain in three years. Members of the Salvadoran death squads and with many trained at the SOA, recruited from the country's impoverished villages and threatened with torture if they didn't join, had a favorite slogan: "Be patriotic, kill a priest."

Beginning with Carter and through the Ronald Reagan years of the 1980s, as much as six billion dollars in weapons would flow to the corrupt and death-dealing Salvadoran government, a major violator of human rights. In the early 1990s, after more than a decade of repression that would see tens of thousands of deaths and displacements, it would be Rep. Joseph Moakley and future Congressman

Jim McGovern who persuaded the House and Senate finally to cut off the military aid.

Reverend Booker comes nearly every semester to the B-CC peace studies classes where his son Andrew was once a member. Days before each visit, the class is prepped by watching *Guns and Greed*, a fact-based documentary, as well by reading excerpts from *Disturbing the Peace: The Story of Father Roy Bourgeois*, which tells the story of Roy Bourgeois and SOA. In the book's foreword, Martin Sheen, who has been arrested sixty-six times at antiwar protests, including one at Fort Benning, hailed the selfless agitator as a man who lived in a weather of grace that was a quickening for all those thousands who came every November. It was, Sheen writes, Roy Bourgeois's "extraordinary reputation as a tireless peace and justice advocate for the poor of Central and South America" that made his years and years of vigilance a singular feat in the American peace movement.

> Dear Pastor Booker:
>
> Your talk was enlightening. I never knew about the school at Fort Benning that trains assassins for Latin American countries. I find it commendable that you protested against the school and even risked arrest and being jailed.
>
> My family is from El Salvador, so learning of the torture and murder in El Salvador that was caused by the United States trainers was shocking.
>
> Hearing about your struggle with depression, substance abuse, and alcoholism but getting through it all and standing up for other people was inspiring.
>
> Thank you so much for coming to speak to our class and sharing your experiences and ideals and enlightening us on a subject we would never have known about.
>
> Sincerely,
> Alexa Gonzalez

Dear Pastor Booker:

Thank you for coming to tell your heroic story. Men and women who serve in the military are heroes but for what you did for Central American refugees is brave and heroic. Do you know that the Democratic National Committee (DNC) made it part of their policy platform to shut down SOA school. There is no need for it. So if Hillary was to be elected president the people's wishes would have been met to having the school shut down. Since Trump is the president-elect and the Republican party has Congress in its pocket, it would be silly to believe that such a thing would happen in the next four years.

But let us not lose faith. I'll hope and pray that Trump and Congress would make the right rather than the wrong choice.

Go with God, Pastor Booker—
Derrick Jones

Dear Pastor Booker:

It is rare to find someone who has the courage of their convictions and act to defend their principles no matter the adverse personal consequences. I am glad to have found such a person in you.

Protest lets us fight back against power. It allows us to voices our values, to show our solidarity, and to force a change. The bravery and willpower it took to do what you did by stepping across the line at the SOA protest is remarkable, especially knowing that you could spend up to six months in prison. I hope to one day garner the courage of protestors like you to join the action on the front lines standing up for progressive ideals.

Sincerely,
Conor Smythe

Dear Pastor Booker:

It astonishes me that a man like you has been to prison. Once I found out that you went there because you were standing up for something you believed in, I held ever more admiration for you. I was surprised to hear that you learned more in three months of prison than you did in three years of being a pastor, but I guess that really says something about getting out there and taking a risk.

You are an inspiring person, and what you said about showing faith and belief through "who you stand with" will certainly stick with me. Thank you for that.

Andrei Pinkus

Dear Pastor Booker:

One thing you said to us really rang true with me: behind every violent action is fear. I think that's true and so relevant in our current situation as a society. We are afraid of change, poverty, guns, terrorists, disease, and so much more.

So what do we do? We fight. We yell. We take up arms. If we could all just take a second to acknowledge that we are all scared maybe we would learn to solve our problems instead of making them worse. I really admire how you have stood up for your beliefs and how far you have gone. Thank you so much for speaking to our class. Your story is inspiring. I hope one day I can have the courage and reasons to take a stand.

Sincerely,
Madison Shaffer

Dear Pastor Booker:

I truly admire your character, your passions and conviction in your own beliefs and morals. As I live, I too will seek to uphold that in which I believe as you have done relentlessly in your work. You have used the power of religion for what I believe it is meant (this said as one who identifies more culturally than spiritually) by bringing people together and creating a safe and sacred community space inclusive of all.

Best,
Janey Fredman

18

WHEN PAUL CHAPPELL, a 2002 graduate of the United States Military Academy at West Point, told his Korean-born that he was leaving the Army after seven years and reaching the rank of captain, she vented: "Are you out of your mind? Nobody is going to hire you. It's bad enough that you look Asian, but you're also part black. Nobody is going to give a job to a black man who looks Asian."

This forecast, bleak as it was but still plausible, didn't pan out. In 2009, Paul's book, *Will War Ever End? A Soldier's Vision of Peace for the 21st Century*, won the attention of officials at the Nuclear Age Peace Foundation in Santa Barbara, California. He was hired as the nonprofit's Peace Leadership director.

On his most recent trip to Washington, he spoke to my classes at Georgetown Law, American University, the University of Maryland and, for sure, once again at B-CC.

If a difference exists between this latest visit and earlier ones, it is the recent publication of his book *The Art of Waging Peace: A Strategic Approach to Improving Our Lives and the World*. With chapter titles that include "How West Point Trained Me for Peace Activism" and "The Deceptive Beauty of War," Chappell's well-honed prose combines autobiography, historical analysis, and reasoned alternatives to military violence. Chappell's personal story of moving from waging war to waging peace places him in the company of past and current icons who believed that moral force and the forces of truth, resistance, and negotiation are superior to and more effective than violent military force. Among them are former warriors Sargent Shriver,

Howard Zinn, Philip Berrigan, Garry Davis, Andy Jacobs, Mark Hatfield, George McGovern, and Francis of Assisi.

Chappell's transition could easily be unlikeliest. His childhood was wracked with violence, both receiving and giving it. Growing up in Alabama in a dysfunctional childhood, he suffered repeated beatings from his half-black half-white father, a veteran of the Korean and Vietnam wars who returned home emotionally scarred by his combat experiences. He suffered paranoia and suicidal and murderous impulses. "Throughout my childhood," Paul writes, "I saw my father lose his grip on reality, and this frightening behavior caused me to struggle with my own sanity. As I grew older, the trauma I inherited from my father caused me to embark on a relentless search for understanding, peace and trust."

Outside the home, where schoolmates bullied him because of his multiethnic background and appearance, he was a troubled student. Occasional outbursts of violence led to a dismissal from an elementary school and a high school suspension. A turning point came in the eighth grade when he asked a teacher, "Where does violence come from?" She said, "Human beings are naturally violent and warlike. War is part of human nature, because people are evil. It is human nature to be greedy, hateful and selfish."

Paul recalls thinking that the answer made no sense, even to his adolescent mind: "If humans are naturally violent and warlike, why does war drive so many people like my father insane? From that point on, I was determined to study war the way a doctor studies an illness."

The Art of Waging Peace is Paul's fourth book. In my B-CC classes, he drew on all of them to ground his argument that violence is a learned behavior and, rather than being natural, it is the opposite. "The most effective way to kill human beings and not experience guilt or remorse," he says, "is to imagine they are not human beings. This involves viewing people as subhuman so we can rationalize the act of killing. Or seeing people as evil monsters so we can perceive the act of killing as a necessary purging of evil from the world."

Pressured by his parents to seek a military career, Paul gained entry to West Point with his strong high school grades and SAT scores. His time at the academy was followed by seven years of sol-diering, including a high-risk posting in Iraq, leading to the con-clusion that "almost everything our society and the media teach us about war is a distortion of the truth."

So began a period of self-education in military history, psy-chology, nonviolence, and empathy. Without West Point and the Army, it is doubtful the introspection would ever have happened. Now thirty-five, Paul is a polished writer and peace educator whose inclusion in the American peace movement is secure. A question he posed to the B-CC classes centered on how people two or three hun-dred years from now will judge us, as we look back and severely con-demn educated and seemingly moral Americans for making it legal to own slaves, denying women the right to own property or vote, for criminalizing racial intermarriage, for prosecuting homosexuals. Will they ask us how it was possible they stockpiled nuclear bombs? How did they let one president after another militarily invade third world countries? Why did they not see that animal agribusiness pol-lution was a major cause of climate warming? Why were they chron-ically indifferent to thousands of people dying of starvation every day around the world—a death every eleven seconds. How did they ignore the cruelty inflicted on animals by the meat, dairy, and egg industries? And why did meat eaters keep paying them to kill billions of chickens, cows, and pigs?

> Dear Paul:
>
> Your visit to our class provided us with a great opportunity for a thought exercise. I think it is vital that we do not just accept the world as it is but to examine it with fresh eyes. Your suggestion that we try to look at contemporary society as if we were someone from the future world reminded me of a similar thought exercise in which you pre-tend to be an alien visiting earth in order to view the world without subconscious preconceived conceptions. Over the weekend, I reflected on your Friday talk and tried to come up with some

aspects of society today, which people in the future might look back on as immoral or backward.

I wonder: what will they think of borders? Why did people spend their time watching TV shows about other people's lives instead of enjoying their own? Why did people not accept the reality of climate change as the greatest threat to our world? Why did nations have nuclear arsenal if they knew that the deployment of one nuke would lead certainly to the destruction of the world? Why did the richest eighty people in the world have more wealth than the bottom half of the world's population? Why did they worship celebrity and gossip rather than science and reason? How did the US call itself a democracy when money so obviously corrupted its political system? Why were drones acceptable? Why was domestic violence punished but foreign military violence encouraged? Why did so many domestic criminals rot in jail while war criminals roam free? Why did so many people seem apathetic in the face of mass surveillance, rising inequality, climate change, nuclear proliferation, refugee crisis, criminal justice, mass exploitation, systemic racism, systemic sexism, religious oppression, bought elections, and corrupt politicians? Why didn't they get a say in all these issues? Why were our economic structures systemically based on domination, oppression, and hierarchy? Why didn't they value mutual aid above mutual destruction? Why did they accept an economic system in which so many are left alienated? Why didn't they govern their own lives instead of allowing the economical politic elite to control us? Why didn't they change?

Your raising questions like this gives me hope in humanity. People can come to understand each other, no matter how worked up they are. We can solve our problems through peace and compassion rather than violence and oppression.

Thank you for opening my mind a little more.

Sincerely,
Conor Smythe

Dear Paul:

Listening to your views and opinions influenced me. I never thought about how we look back and question why people did things. I bet America will look back on our lives and question why we did some of the stuff we are doing.

I also don't get why we treat dogs with more respect than cows or pigs. I hope that one day all animals will be treated with respect.

Thank you so much for coming and taking time to teach us.

Marley Clendenin

Dear Paul:

Thank you for exposing our class to a new way of thinking about the current state of our society. It is not often that we think about how our society will be viewed by future generations. I believe that people will look back at this generation with scrutiny over practices we don't think twice about.

Thank you for this new perspective. I'm sure it will not only change my worldview but that of others in the class.

Sincerely,
Sydney Jesus-Allen

Dear Paul:

Most people have ideas but can't verbalize them. You have the invaluable skill of speech. Everything you said yesterday rang true with our class. Thank you so much for coming in to see us. You gave us a lot to think about. I agree with you that animal cruelty will one day be looked back on us as an unthinkable evil. I really enjoyed how you used so many specific examples and dates in your discussion. I hope that one day I can study more about peace and be familiar with all the people and events you described. I applaud your dedication to peace and your positivity. Thank you again!

Sincerely,
Madison Shaffer

Dear Paul:

You forced me to think deep thoughts yesterday. I still don't quite know how I would have convinced a Harvard graduate of 1800 that women deserve equal rights.

As a half-Asian, like you, I also find it difficult at times to fit in with those around me. Obviously, though, there is more hope now in 2016 to fit in than during the time in which you grew up. So much has changed in so few years. Thank you so much, Paul.

Sincerely,
Antonio Ramirez

Dear Paul:

It was an absolute pleasure hearing you speak about the positive progression of the country over the past few generations. The scenarios you presented us with challenged me to look into the roots of the issues that once plagued our country. Further, I always love hearing about vegetarianism and veganism (I too am a vegetarian) and the ways people to make that change in their lives.

Thank you for all you do to promote a peaceful society.

Sincerely,
Celia Goldfarb

19

SINCE 1987, B-CC has had seven principals. Why so many? A story is told that when state officials make routine visits to speak to teachers, staff, and students by way of accrediting the school, they find that all is well. Sparklingly well. Except for one major problem: B-CC parents act as if they are coprincipals.

Donna Redmond Jones, a former English and journalism high school teacher in Richmond who majored in English and psychology at the University of Virginia and then earned a doctorate from the University of Maryland, was the principal for six years at the Rosa Parks Middle School in Montgomery County before being appointed head of school at B-CC.

The June 4, 2016, *Washington Post* reported that Ms. Jones "had told students for months that if they drank or used drugs at the prom they would lose their chance to participate in commencement." Jones disciplined six seniors who drank. "But as the June 1 graduation day approached, interim superintendent Larry A. Bowers overturned Jones's decision to bar them from graduation."

True to Montgomery County form, a windstorm of opinions quickly gusted on the decisions of the principal and superintendent. I sided with Ms. Jones. Her disciplinary purpose was to save lives, those of students who kill themselves by driving with alcohol coursing through their bloodstreams. According to federal figures, approximately two thousand teenagers die in car crashes annually, with a third involving alcohol. As someone who has held firm to my vow in high school never to consume alcohol, I do all I can to persuade my students to take a stand, first, to deny the alcohol industry its money and, second, if they do drink to look into their hearts to ask what in their lives is so empty that the alcohol drug is needed to fill it.

I've never known a family that didn't have a life ruined because of drinking, whether a parent, grandparent, or relative. It's a highly addictive drug, which is why I reject the drink-in-moderation argument. It's the same as telling children to play moderately with fire or teenagers to drive moderately above the speed limit. The Georgetown University Center on Alcohol Marketing and Youth reports that the typical teenager will have seen more than one hundred thousand beer commercials before turning eighteen. The goal of the loathsome companies is brand loyalty. Research shows that once a person connects emotionally with a particular brand of beer, that loyalty remains in place for life. A recent study revealed that 77 percent of teenagers took up drinking by the end of twelfth grade.

So yes, Sister Jones: good show.

When the new principal came to the peace studies classes to speak and to listen, the students' appreciation was nearly unanimous.

Dear Dr. Jones:

When you first came into my peace studies class yesterday, I was nervous. I'm not sure why, but I was waiting to be yelled at or spoken down to. Instead, you surprised me. You sat down and had a civil, open conversation with us. I really appreciate your desire for feedback and how accepting you were of my classmates' suggestions. I think having open discussions about drugs and alcohol are important—especially for seniors who are headed off to college next year. The way the recent assembly on alcohol abuse went many people were angry and upset. So I am glad you were open to our feedback. I also think it is important that the principals have a relationship with their students. Your coming into class yesterday built the relationship. So thank you for listening to us.

Mallory Mical

Dear Dr. Jones:

As high schoolers, we often think we are immune, that nothing bad will happen to us. However, this is not the case, for we have all seen friends and family members corrupted by doing drugs and alcohol, and it is important that we don't abuse it.

Thank you for taking the time and putting so much effort into our safety. There is this culture around drugs and drinking, especially the mentality that you need alcohol to have a good time. This may seem shallow, but in the mind of a high schooler, it presents a huge conflict, especially when friends are doing it, which can be hard to ignore. I look forward to more discussions about this issue.

Thanks for your support—

Sincerely,
Corinne Chapman

Dear Dr. Jones:

After this past weekend, having to help a friend out when she was in trouble, it was relieving to know you are reaching out to get our advice.

School dances are always fun, but it is devastating to know or hear about a classmate getting transported to the hospital. It's sad to think that getting wasted is considered a social norm, and I know there is no way to actually stop underage drinking however—much people need to learn their limits.

I appreciate your reaching out to us as our principal and for truly caring about us and our safety.

Cindy Pontachack

Dear Dr. Jones:

I'm really glad that you've taken such a strong stance against drugs and alcohol. Both are dangerous in the B-CC community. It's never a popular position to take with high schoolers, but it's an important one. Students need to know that their actions have real consequences. I'd also like to thank you genuinely listening to our input. I could tell that you were actually taking our ideas into consideration.

I can promise you now that I will never do drugs. Take this as my pledge.

Thank you so much,
Eve Chesivoir

Dear Dr. Jones:

A lot of people probably groan when they hear our principle is coming in to talk about drug abuse, but it's obviously an important issue that needs to be addressed. I thank you for understanding that and working hard to emphasize the dangers of drug abuse. I myself lost someone close to me because of overdrinking, and after that day, I swore to never drink or experiment with drugs. I never realized how serious these meetings were until I lost someone, and I am elated that you are trying your best to convey the message as well as get our input on how to do so.

Thank you for visiting our class. Please come back anytime, it keeps us on the right track.

Francisco Morrison

20

A S A HISTORY major at the University of North Carolina, Kurt Newman wasn't overly concerned what he would be doing with that kind of degree. Besides, other issues needed to be heeded—like rooting for the school's basketball team when it took on the Duke powerhouse. The future? Well, stay calm and think about that sometime tomorrow—or the next day and the day after that.

One summer, needing to earn a few dollars, Kurt found a summer job as a hospital orderly—totally unsuspecting it would be life changing. Being among nurses, doctors and sick people awakened him to "the human side of medicine." Around the same time, he recalled to a medical reporter, "I had to have my thyroid removed. It turned out to be cancer, and the impact of that experience with my surgeon changed my view of surgery."

Today Kurt Newman, sixty-four, is the president and CEO of the Children's National Medical Center, Washington, DC, a 303-bed haven of mercy and competence that employs 5,400 people and a revenue of $875 million in 2010, the year before the former history major took over.

After medical school at Stanford University and residencies, Dr. Neman began a practice in pediatric surgery at Children's in 1984. His work often took him to the neonatal intensive care rooms where he met his wife, Alison. They married in 1992 and have two sons, Robert and Jack. Both were in the peace studies classes.

Relaxed and easygoing, Dr. Newman told stories ranging from operating on a boy with a bloated colon to helping operate on a fourteen-year-old girl shot in the chest at a DC playground by plugging whole in the child's heart with his finger. She survived. Some twenty years later she wrote to thank him for saving her life.

What resonated with many students was Dr. Newman's counsel, based on the curves and twists on his pathways through high school and college to becoming a surgeon and head of Children's National.

> Dear Dr. Newman:
>
> Every year I run the Children's Hospital 5K with my field hockey team at B-CC and every year I've loved doing it, despite my hatred of running.
>
> Being a second semester senior and going off to college next year, it's a little nerve-wracking thinking about what we want to pursue in the future. You really got us to thinking about just doing what we seem is fun, and it will all work out in the end with real hard work and dedication. You did major in history and look where you are now. The hospital does such great work and impacts our community heavily. Thank you for all the work you've done and continue to do and for speaking to our class.
>
> All the best,
> Cindy Pontachack

> Dear Dr. Newman:
>
> The funny stories you shared and delightful insights about college life and beyond really changed my perspective. I haven't really thought of a plan for my future quite yet and you said it was okay for us not to. I've always heard that "if you don't have a plan you're screwed, so come up with one."

You were just a living, breathing example of how you don't have to have everything figured out, that it will eventually come you if you are open-minded.

Thanks again,
Sammy Baydasin

Dear Dr. Newman:

Thank you so much for taking the time out of your busy work day to impart your wisdom to us. I was shocked when you told us that you didn't even get into the premed track until after your first year at UNC. I was under the impression that you had to start early in medicine otherwise you would never make it to med school.

As you may know, I am interested in the field of medicine and hearing a story like yours only makes me more excited for the infinite possibilities that lie ahead.

Thank you once again; hopefully, we can talk again.

Sincerely
Jack Colbert

Dear Dr. Newman:

Your story on how you came to be where you are now was an eye-opener for me. I want to become a doctor, though I am not sure which field I should study since I find a lot of them to be interesting.

When I am not sure of what is to come I feel anxious, but if things don't really go the way you planned, sometimes it may lead you somewhere entirely different.

So I thank you for taking time your time to come to our class.

Sincerely,
Jenicka Jordan

Dear Dr. Newman:

I really enjoyed hearing about your lovely experience with the megacolon. I hope to have stories like that of my own one day. Don't get me wrong, that sounds nasty, but I really want to be a trauma surgeon one day. Hearing your story made me more hopeful for my future. You overcame the odds of starting later than everyone else, and now you're the president of Children's Hospital.

I've learned that if you want to do something, if you have that calling, it is possible. Thank you so much for telling us your story. You've really helped me believe in myself.

Sincerely,
Eve Chesivour

Dear Dr. Newman:

My family has been to Children's Hospital quite a lot. I used to have this funky foot disorder, and I traveled doctor to doctor to figure out what to do. We did Botox in my calves, castings, and three tendon lengthening surgeries. Children's Hospital was one of my stops. Additionally, my friend was diagnosed with cancer around five years ago now. She is officially rid of it as of a year ago, but during her years there, she battled it. That was for coming to our class where she was.

Thank you so much for coming to my class. People like you are the reason my friend is alive and I can walk properly.

All the best,
Becca Dorn

21

TWO MONTHS BEFORE Jean Manes was at the US State Department on March 17, 2016, being sworn in as ambassador to El Salvador, she came to the peace studies classes. Among the visuals she brought were a small pile of her passports—dozens of pages stamped at ports of entries in well over fifty countries where she had traveled since the early 1990s as a foreign service worker posted in Syria, Argentina, Uruguay, Portugal, Brazil, Afghanistan. For three years, after working from 1992 to 1999 at the US Information Agency, she toiled in the White House organizing presidential trips abroad which included making accommodations for the press corps. Hundreds of thousands of miles brought her to at least sixty countries.

Jean Manes graduated from Highland Christian Academy kindergarten in Florida in 1976 and its high school in 1988. She went on to earn a degree in foreign policy in 1992 from Liberty University and a master's degree in international administration from American University in 1996. She entered the game as an intern at the Senate Foreign Relations Committee chaired by Sen. Claiborne Pell, and eventually being supported by Barack Obama, who made her the ambassador to El Salvador. At the swearing in, she gave thanks, among many others, to her grandmother Alice: "Her side of the family has a Choctaw Indian heritage, and I am honored to wear a traditional necklace created by Tia Carter that is the style worn by Choctaw women." She acknowledged the realities she would be facing in El Salvador, "from gang violence to a stagnant economy to corruption."

On July 4, 2016, a story in *The Washington Post* with a San Salvador dateline offered some details that can only be called horrific and chilling about daily life in the nation of three million. It began: "After becoming the world's murder capital last year and posting an equally bloody start to 2016, this violence-torn Central American nation has seen its monthly homicide rate fall by about half." Why the drop? The Salvadoran government attributes it to "a tough military counteroffensive against the country powerful gangs, deploying a special security force and transferring imprisoned organized-crime leaders to a maximum-security lockup to isolate them. But the gangs also claim credit. The three main groups—the Mara Salvatrucha, Barrio 18 Revolucionarios, and Barrio 18 Surenos—forged a non-aggression pact in March to try reduce the killings... Either way, killings in El Salvador dropped from 611 in March to 353 in April and 351 in May. There were 331 homicides in July, compared with 677 in the same month in 2015."

More news still, this from The New York Times July 15, 2016, relating to the 1980s when death squads and military assassins were killings machines: "In a ruling that clears the way for El Salvador to prosecute the perpetrators of war crimes committed during the brutal civil war, the country's highest court has struck down an amnesty law that has protected soldiers, rebel fighters and death squads for more than two decades."

Whatever gifts of resilience, amity, and diplomacy Ambassador Manes may have, they will be as needed in El Salvador as they are tested.

Dear Jean Manes:

While you were talking to our class, all I could think about was my mom. She grew up in a small town in northern Wisconsin surrounded by farms and cows. She knew that she wanted to be a foreign affairs correspondent when she was young, and she dreamed of traveling all around the world. So she paid her way through college with a journalism major and ended up in Costa

Rica working with the Peace Corps. My mom traveled throughout Latin America and lived in Costa Rica for three years and Nicaragua for three more.

She ended up coming back to the US to be with my dad. Now she is a stay-at-home mom with three kids.

You succeeded in a lot of people's dreams. Everyone wants to travel see the world. Your career is inspiring. I thank you for sharing it with us!

Sincerely,
Madison Shaffer

Dear Jean Manes:

We enjoyed your visit to our class. Being from El Salvador, it was really special having you in my class. Having a job that allows you to travel and to know new cultures is something that I've always dreamed of, but it's not easy, as you said. But I see you handle this job with a passion and grace.

I had the chills hearing your story about the time you slept in a sleeping bag guarded by drunk men. Sounds like adventure has followed you everywhere.

Thank you for coming,
Micelle

22

ZAMBIA, A LANDLOCKED republic on the plateaus of Southern Africa that regained its independence from Britain in 1964 and where nearly 70 percent of the population subsists below the poverty line, was a longtime host to the Peace Corps when Lauren Kovach came as a volunteer. She served from July 2012 to August 2014 in the village of Chanjowe Chadiza in the Eastern Province. Her path to the English-speaking nation of twelve million citizens began after graduating as an A student from the University of Maryland in 2009 with a degree in landscape architecture. She found work for three years with a multidisciplinary design firm but then, adventurous and with a touch of fearlessness, she took leave and traveled to Sao Tome and Principe, the Portuguese island nation off the equatorial coast of West Africa for a five-week program in drawing run by the Maryland Institute College of Art.

Self-immersing in the culture, art, and history of a land that probably not one American in a thousand had even faint knowledge of was enough to change the direction of her life.

In a recent essay, she wrote: "After about a month in a country with derelict or nonexistent sidewalks, upon returning I found myself in front of a computer detailing plans to renovate the University of Rochester's perfectly fine asphalt pathway into concrete walks with granite edging. One week after returning from Sao Tome I applied to the Peace Corps."

"Some of my best in-country times," she wrote of her time in Zambia, "were spent in the first three months getting to know the culture, language and my assignment. There's nothing quite as satisfying as hands-on learning or as liberating getting to know likeminded people. During my two years, I attempted to start a number of projects that failed, or fizzled without my continuously supporting them: adult-ed classes, a food processing club and a school garden. I helped a community group get funding for a piggery which we built together and which ran for the past two years. My enduring lesson regarding international development was that it usually does not work. But it's also not fair or ethical to withhold a chance for a person or group, so you have to try. About the USA, I learned to be a bit more patriotic. America has its shortfalls but it felt good to be representing a country that is working to bring opportunity to others."

Dear Lauren:

I have a burning question: are those dried fish you passed around during your talk actually eaten dried or did you just dry them out for preservative purposes? Praise to you if you ate them dried. I'm not a picky eater, but I don't think I could do that.

That aside, thank you so much for sharing your stories about the Peace Corps. I think it's the most selfless thing you could do. People always feel bad for "the starving kids in Africa," but you actually did something about it. You've really made me want to do something about it too.

Thank you so much,
Eve Chesivoir

Dear Lauren:

I can say honestly: "We need more people like you!" In a world where the most important thing is being successful or rich, there are incredible people like you who want to help others and a better and peaceful society. You're changing the world and the way many people think about what we must do to live in an equalized community.

Congratulations, you touched my heart!

Jaime Silva

Dear Lauren:

Thank you for coming to our class to talk to us about your experience in Zambia. I have always wanted to learn more about the Peace Corps. Your stories really resonated with me. I have gone on many service trips: one to Ghana, three to the Dominican Republic, so I was interested in the Peace Corps program. Your stories were interesting, and I appreciate your being honest with us by saying how uncomfortable you were at times. After you spoke to us, I really want to join the Peace Corps and get out of the "Bethesda Bubble."

I think it's so cool how you get to train/learn the language and be able to travel while helping people. I know you mentioned you wanted to go back and visit, so I really hope you get to do that.

Thanks again!

Mallory Mical

Dear Lauren:

I want to tell you how amazingly relatable and engaging your talk was to our class yesterday. You could have been preachy, but instead you focused on your own journey and people that you interacted with and helped while in Zambia. I think that the human component is ultimately what being in the Peace Corps should be about. Your sense of humor and clear passion for this experience was incredible. I respect you as the brave and kind member of humanity that you are.

You've actually inspired me to consider joining the Peace Corps, so thank you for that. Keep changing lives.

Thanks,
Nate Fellner

Dear Lauren:

Hearing your story has made me want to take a service trip. Your experience has inspired me to open my eyes to the world and has changed my perspective on global economic inequality. I used to think I wanted to major in sports management, but now I think I am more interested in majoring is something like community service.

The first story you told about the native women is something I'll never forget. I think it is extremely important to experience situations that make you feel vulnerable and out of place because that is the only way to truly experience something. Thank you for coming to our class and I hope to hear more from you.

Grace Rosen

Dear Lauren:

Your time in the Peace Corps seemed like such a great learning experience. Although the reality in transitioning in Zambia was rough and different, you showed us that it is a really rewarding experience. Personally, I had been thinking about joining the Peace Corps after college while talking about it in class, but after hearing and listening to you, it really encouraged me more to want to join.

Thank you, and I wish you the best.

Allie Vasquez

Dear Lauren:

I was really excited to hear that you would be coming to our class. Two summers ago I went on a service trip to Paraguay and worked with a Peace Corps volunteer in a small remote farming village. The experience deeply affected my perspective not only on poverty and our Western countries but on my life in the US as well.

I really appreciate you describing your experiences in Zambia and also how you felt when you returned home because I had experienced similar albeit smaller readjustments to American life. It was nice to hear from someone else who put into words something that is difficult for me to explain.

Thank you for visiting our class.

Sincerely,
Riley Pfaff

23

A HIGH POINT OF every semester is a field trip of about three hundred yards east from the high school on the sidewalk of East-West Highway to the School of Life Ashram. For more than two decades it has been a commune committed to karma yoga meditation and spiritual development. The community of seven members, whose garb is all white and diet is vegetarian, is led by Vyasa, a Peru-born bearded guru and a model of kindness who has welcomed class after class for first- and second-period forty-minute visits. Self-supporting, the early-rising members include two former Peace Corps volunteers—Togo and the Solomon Islands—and three members who are adjunct professors teaching yoga classes at American University and George Washington University.

The Ashram hosts lecture programs and meditation classes Friday and Saturday evenings and works with an organic biodynamic farmer in southeast Pennsylvania who grows vegetables and fruits that are marketed every Wednesday at the commune to more than one hundred Bethesda families. On Sundays the members bring a van brimming with food for homeless men and women at Franklin Square in downtown Washington.

It has been a rare student who has left the Ashram unmoved by the warmth, honesty, and humble spirituality of the commune members—genuine communists—and see it as a sanctuary of peace. Before speaking to the class, Vyasa leads the students in singing John Lennon's "Imagine." He calls on Durga, an Ashram member for seventeen years and an accomplished acoustic guitar player, to help raise the voices with her best chords.

Dear Guru Vyasa and fellow Communists:

My future was decided at birth. I was to attend a respected college and with the hard-earned degree lock down a high-paying office job so I can be respected by my peers. Although this path is a cliché, it is one the youth of my upbringing aspire to fulfill. In the commune, it appears you have freed yourselves from the societal pressures of gaining approval through status. I was under the impression I had to travel by land and sea to meet good people like you. It is reassuring to find an enlightened group in Bethesda itself. I strive for what you have obtained.

Sincerely,
Tommy Witkop

Dear Guru Vyasa and Community:

You all look so healthy and pure. If that's what yoga does, please sign me up! I loved singing with you guys and feeling connected to my classmates through that. I also really enjoyed our five-minute meditation. I realized I am harboring a lot of hatred and anger toward people who are just trying to be happy, and this made me feel more compassion than I have felt in a long time.

Sorry, I cannot help out at the soup kitchen this Saturday, but I will try to come at some point soon. As you know, there's something rewarding about making other people's lives better. Thank you for making my day.

Love,
Naomi Gross

Dear Ashram Friends:

The energy I experienced in your home was unlike anything I've felt before. I immediately felt welcome and at peace. You all do such a beautiful job of sharing your spiritual knowledge with others, and I'm so thankful we got to sing and be in such an uplifting space. It was incredibly inspiring to witness how spirituality and the teachings of great minds can influence every part of daily life.

I hope to one day be able to live as consciously as you all do, and to find a place of community and understanding amid the chaos of our society.

Thank you again for inviting us into your beautiful home.

Sincerely,
Isabel Brown

Dear Guru and fellow communists:

Visiting your home last Friday was an intriguing experience. Although I am not religious myself, seeing how spirituality and belief can bring people together in a strong community was fascinating. I have never seen a community quite like yours. Seeing your warmth and trust for others helped opened my mind to the possibility of the spread of communal living like yours, where members share their money, trust each other, and find peace together.

The song that you started by having us sing with you was inspiring. It gave me hope that more people could share the values of peace trust and love that you so clearly display. Also, I appreciate that you passed out the Jill Stein flyer. She is

OPENING MINDS, STIRRING HEARTS

not only the most peace-centered candidate but also the most people-centered.

Thanks for your hospitality.

Conor Smythe

Dear Ashram Brothers and Sisters:

As a graduating senior, I am often feeling stressed and overworked. But when my peace studies class joined you for a morning of reflection and cogitation, I truly felt an overwhelming sense of calm immersing me. As Vyasa asked everyone to breathe in and then breathe out, each breath of air removed my agitation and elicited a newfound tranquility—a feeling desperately needed against the prospect of looming exams.

The environment you all have created in your commune highlights the idea of community to me, one that brings together different groups that interact with each other's lives. Your commune is the epitome of peace. You are all hospitable and amiable, smiling and laughing, composed, and all wearing white—the white, to me, is the reflection of the tabula rasa and your perspective of the world.

When you urged my class to sing "Imagine," I didn't feel pressure—and I loathe singing songs. It felt like a natural response to the kindness all of you emitted—and I actually ended up enjoying myself! The space you have created lacks the prejudice and judgment sometimes found in my school and larger community. The immense respect you have for all humans and their need for love and understanding is highlighted in your charity work. I am very impressed by your work with the homeless who are often overlooked and neglected. I am sure your relationship with them brightens their day and makes them feel less isolated and one with the world.

Sometimes I feel like a loner too. Although my loneliness is nothing compared with that of the homeless people you help.

I would like to say thank you—for making me feel like a friend, and a loved one, during my brief time in your home.

Best wishes,
Elizabeth Stephens

Dear Guru and Community:

I appreciate that you let all of us into your home with open arms. I enjoyed listening to your ways of living at the Ashram and admired all your dedication to create inner peace. I very much agree that world peace starts with inner peace, and I am glad that there are people like you who are helping to contribute to a more peaceful world. I appreciate and respect all of you and what you stand for and the ways you all help the community.

Thank you for offering us yoga and other classes free of charge. I plan to take you up on that offer. Thanks again for everything you do.

Much love,
Brigitte Freeman

Dear Guru and Community:

Thank you so much for welcoming us into your home. You made us feel welcome the second we sat own. In fact, you got some people in our class to sing who don't ever speak in class.

I admire your dedication to peace and helping others.

I've tried meditating, but my mind is too hectic. I wish I could clear it and take time to relax, but in this society and at this school, it seems impossible. I plan to come to one of your classes once my sports season ends.

I look forward to seeing you again! Thank you for all that you taught us.

Sincerely,
Madison Shaffer

Dear Ashram Friends:

When I walked into your home just a block away from my school, I was overcome with a sense of peace and tranquility. Your spiritual center had a calming energy that I was thankful to be a part of during my busy high school day. Thank you for hosting my peace studies class. The meditation you led truly had a lasting impact on my day. I have limited yoga and meditation experiences, but now I am inspired to continue yoga again and start practicing meditation—something I have been meaning to do for a long time.

I consider myself to be a bit of an anxious person, and I am glad I had the experience of coming to the School of Life. Your stories and songs were inspiring, and I am grateful I had the opportunity to take a step back from the stresses in my life and welcome the calm and soothing environment your home provided.

Best,
Penny Saltzman

24

LOS GATOS, A California community of thirty thousand, is ranked the nation's thirtieth wealthiest town by Bloomberg Business. It is home to Netflix in Silicon Valley. It is where John Steinbeck wrote *The Grapes of Wrath*. Los Gatos—"the cats"—is traced to the wariness of Spanish conquistadores to the bobcats and cougars in the local Santa Cruz mountains. The town was immortalized by Woody Guthrie in his enduring folksong "Deportee." In the 1950s when a rickety airplane carrying twenty-eight migrant workers back to Mexico blew up over Los Gatos Canyon, the media said, "they were just deportees."

Joan Baez, Bruce Springsteen, Emmylou Harris, Johnny Cash, Bob Dylan, Dolly Parton, and Woody's son Arlo are among the artists who have sung "Deportee." The lyrics are worth taking a look at, haunting as they are and as relevant as they are to our own times when contemptible politicians pledge to build walls on the southern borders and ship back the "illegals."

> The crops are all in and the peaches are is rott'ning
> The oranges piled in their creosote dumps;
> They're flying 'em back to the Mexico border
> To pay all their money to wade back again.
>
> Goodbye to my Juan, goodbye Rosalita,
> Adios mis amigo, Jesus y Maria;

You won't have a name when you ride the big
airplane,
And they will call you will be "deportees"

My father's own father, he waded that river,
They took all the money he made in his life;
My brothers and sisters came working the fruit trees
And they rode the truck till they lay down and died

Some of us are illegal, and some are not wanted,
Our work contract's out and we've got to move on;
Six hundred miles to that Mexican border,
They chase us like outlaws, like rustlers, like
thieves.

We died in your hills and we've died on your
deserts
We died in your valleys, we've died in your plains
We died 'neath your trees and we died in your
bushes
Both sides of that river, we died just the same

The sky plane caught fire over Los Gatos Canyon,
A fireball of lightning, and shook all our hills
Who are all these friends, all scattered like dry
leaves?
The radio says, "They are just deportees."

Is this the best way we can grow our big orchards?
Is this the best way we can grow our good fruit?
To fall like dry leaves to rot on my topsoil
And be called by no name except "deportees"?

Los Gatos is where Brandy Pech was raised. At eighteen, she traveled east to study in the School of International Service at American University from which she graduated in 2014 with a focus on International Peace and Conflict Resolution in Africa. Pursuing a master's, she is working as a program coordinator for the Executive and International Studies Program.

Brandy was a star student in my Alternatives to Violence course in 2013. She was ever gracious in our class discussions, wrote literate papers, and had a caring heart. She also suffered depression. When Brandy spoke to the peace studies classes at B-CC about her illness, she was among the estimated 350 million people globally who endure depression. It is an illness that can twin with phobias, alcohol abuse, emotional or social withdrawal, prolonged sadness, anxiety, ongoing lethargy, feelings of pessimism, indifference to the needs of others.

In the United States, according to the National Institutes for Mental Health, 11 percent of adolescents experience depression by eighteen. Thirty percent of college students reported feeling depressed, of kind that drained them of the energy to stay involved with their academic or social lives.

Little time was needed for the B-CC students to feel both empathy and admiration for Brandy as she spoke about her illness and her seeking medical help much the way she would go to an orthopedist if she had a broken ankle or a dermatologist if she had a skin rash. She pointedly wondered why many people who suffer depression see themselves as failures or feel shame when they would not feel defeated if they had a case of tennis elbow or a weak meniscus from too much running. Why is mental illness cast into the shadows the way physical disabilities never are?

In their letters of appreciation, several students confided that were in a depression and that Brandy's openness was door that might be the opening to recovery.

> Dear Brandy:
> It is amazing to hear how much you have overcome, and how you still are fighting with mental illness. I appreciated how much you opened up to us. It made others struggling with things similar feel like they are not alone. I have always hated the stigma on mental illness

and think the more it is talked about the more informed others will be. So thank you so much for coming to talk with us.

Love,
Zoe Persons

Dear Brandy:

It was brave of you to talk your depression because not a lot of people can do that. I'm glad you received help when you did and you can maintain your depression. You are very beautiful, and you don't need to be going through this, but I will keep you in my prayers and hopefully soon you won't have to take medicine anymore.

Life is too short, and I hope you become the teacher you want to be.

Unsigned

Dear Brandy:

What you taught us through your lecture were some of the most important things we have learned all year. In high school, if you aren't diagnosed yourself with anxiety or depression, you probably know someone who is. I happen to know many people suffering from the same illness you have, and sometimes I do not know what to say or how to understand their issues when they feel anxious or depressed. The lessons you gave us and the stories you told us were insights into what it means to struggle the way you did. It allowed us to understand these disorders in a whole new way.

I appreciate it so much that you took the time to come speak to our class and so grateful for the knowledge I now have about anxiety and depression.

I hope the flexible hours of your job prove to be helpful!

Thanks again,
Henry Greenblatt

Dear Brandy:

Depression is more present in our culture than anyone would like to admit. Even though it is eating away at so many young teens, our schools don't like to talk about it. They sidestep the subject because they know they are one of the main causes: AP classes, Ivy League schools, SATs, ACT, tests, quizzes, and essays. It takes people that are brave enough to speak up, like yourself, to force our society to acknowledge this issue.

I hope you continue healing and wish the best of luck at your job. You have come so far and done so well. I know you will continue to rise.

Sincerely,
Madison Shaffer

25

I CAME TO KNOW Amr Farouki when he was one of three males among seventeen females in my Peace and Social Justice course at American University where he would graduate in 2016 with degrees in International Relations and Finance. He was also the only Arab American in the class. He was all I could ask for in a student: engaged, outgoing, a sterling listener, and easygoing when I ribbed him about his friendship with skydiving King Abdullah of Jordan. Amr, born in Washington, grew up in a liberal Jordanian family in Amman. He was educated at King's Academy, in what he calls "a private American-style boarding school dubbed 'Deerfield of the desert.' My parents heavily concentrated on affording us the best education possible. Since the best schools in Jordan are international ones that follow English-based curricula, they emphasize mastering my mother tongue, Arabic. If we don't immerse ourselves in our own culture and heritage, then how can we understand another? The only way to close the gap between people is to realize that when we cut through all the differences in opinion and lifestyles, we are humans and find daily struggles in the same places. We are all inherently the same."

Turning eighteen, Amr returned to Washington to enrol in American University. In my class, as well as in his talk to the B-CC students, Amr argued that while American television doesn't show it, people of the Arab world are just like people of the West. They fall in love, they savor music, and they practice religion. "Connections among humans transcend borders and governments. American University has given me hope of being able to close the gap."

A few days after Amr spoke to the two B-CC classes, I asked for his reflections on how it all went. "That morning," he said, "astonished me. It was not that the students seemed receptive or respectful, it was their desire to understand the life of the 'other' that truly made me happy. Anyone in the room could see that they were truly passionate about learning. That talk gave me hope that we are able to bridge existing differences. There is no need for war or violence against people on the same earth. All there needs to be is dialogue between people. I truly believe that if there is one lesson we taught that day, it is not to be passive, not to adopt the opinions of others without second-guessing or thinking it in your heart deep down, you truly believe so. Travel the world and make your own assumptions and judge people. But not until you have seen how they live and what influences them."

Amr asked if he could bring one of his close friends—Abdallah Mohammad Ibrahim Abu-Sheikh—to the class. When both came, it turned out to be a double blessing.

Abdallah, the oldest of eight children in an Amman, Jordan family, earned a BA in International Business, Finance, and Banking at Dalhousie University in 2015. "We grew up," he recalled, "learning that Islam is love and peace to all creations be it animals, trees, or people of any race, faith, or color. Islam taught me that it is prohibited to discriminate people according to anything other than their actions."

As with Amr, Abdallah was emotionally moved by his time with the classes: "Although I have spoken at different universities before I came to B-CC, I was never so touched by the reactions of people, as those students sat down and listened with passion and care to every word we had to say, although they came from various backgrounds, ethnicities, and social circles, all shared the same interests and concerns. If there was one thing that I feel I left those students, it's that they not to be passive about anything that goes on around them and to always seek the truth. The bigger part, though, is that I feel like those students touched me in the way that they made me feel like it is from right there that can make a difference educating young men and women like them."

After graduating from American University, Amr moved to Dubai to serve as a financial consultant for some fashion-industry startups. In the fall of 2016, his plans included moving to Palo Alto, California, to work for venture capital firms. Abdallah, with experience as the CEO of a Middle East airline, has settled in Dubai and registered as an investment consultant that has quickly attracted several Fortune 500 companies and three government seeking expertise in renewable energy and power sources.

When Amr returned to Washington in early February 2017, he called to say hello. With two new groups of peace studies students, I invited Amr for a return visit. "I'll come," he said. Like a long-distance runner, he covered much ground. He offered facts. In recent years, Jordan was the third-largest recipient of US military at $500 million, after Israel ($3 billion) and Egypt ($1.3 billion). Due to the progressive and humane politics of King Abdullah, Jordan has spent $2.5 billion on Syrian refugees, in contrast to the paranoid policies of the Trump administration. More facts: the country has no oil reserves. Water is scarce. His opinions ranged from criticism of the United States, military interventions in the Middle East, to the reality that many Americans lack an understanding about Islam, an intellectual deficit traceable to not reading the Koran as well as not getting past media stereotypes of the Arab culture. He praised the uprisings in US cities against the Trump administration travel bans of Muslims. He advised students to think about taking a college semester in Jordan, guaranteeing that it would be totally worthwhile.

Dear Amr:
    I had preconceived notions of Jordan. I'm not racist or xenophobic, but I am pro-Israel because I am Jewish. So I was used to thinking of Jordan as another "one of those" violent countries bordering Israel that opposes its very existence. When I was in Israel, I almost crossed over into Jordan by accident, and that was terrifying. I was always taught that the Middle East is violent

and anti-Isreal. Learning that Jordan is actually quite progressive is fascinating.

Thank you for humanizing your country.

Sincerely
Rebecca Schrader

Dear Amr:

Here in our Bethesda bubble we have such a limited perspective on world events, especially about the Middle East. Having you speak in our peace studies class was the perfect eye-opener into the happenings in Jordan and your view of the United States. Your advice to read a variety of news sources was so important. As high schoolers and Bethesda residents, we too often insist that our views and opinions are the only accurate ones. But you taught us that issues are never as simple as good and bad or as clear-cut as we think. As someone who plans to pursue politics and government, your talk was a welcome reminder amid tough times that the humanitarian approach is always more important than the political one.

Thank you so much for speaking to us. I will carry your lessons with me for years to come.

Cate Paterson

Dear Amr:

The American political environment right now is horrific. We have a racist and cruel president who plans to take detrimental actions in the next four years. One of those actions is what people refer to as "the Muslim ban." Living in Bethesda, I don't have a lot of interaction with those who are Muslim. Most people I encounter are Catholic or Jewish. I myself was raised Catholic, but I find myself being drawn by so many kinds of religions. I heavily appreciate your coming in and discussing your faith with us, and to help clarify how it can be interpreted. I think that many people are wildly uninformed, but people like you who explain it beautifully bring more understanding and communication, which are the recipes for world peace.

I thank you for that.

Maria Neas

Dear Amr:

The only times I've ever been near Jordan are my trips to Israel. Other than the desert landscape, which I've seen in Israel, I can't imagine what it's like growing up in a country like Jordan with few natural resources like oil and water.

The life I've grown up with seems so unfair—living in a suburban home with ample space, a television on each floor of the house, internet access, and showers that I can extend as long as I want. Sometimes I wish I'd grown up with less, so I wouldn't have so many selfish, American expectations. Maybe a simpler life is better.

Either way, thank you so much for coming into our class to share your story. I will definitely continue in the weeks to come to keep thinking about the points brought up about Jordan and the United States.

Sincerely,
Rebecca Boden

Dear Amr:

Thank you for enlightening the class about American intervention in the Middle East. As someone who has Lebanese friends, I had heard most of your arguments already. However, I was skeptical about them until you spoke to the class yesterday. By sharing your personal experiences with us, I thank you, as they helped me understand the severity of American interventions in the Middle East and how we are diverted from it by the media.

By tackling the issue of extremism within Islam in a predominantly American Christian country, you have shown incredible courage and have pushed me to go further to not only defend and support Islam in discussions but to advocate and stand up for it.

Thank you,
Marco Casanova

Several letters were to both Amr and Abdallah:

Dear Amr and Abdullah:

I'm very thankful that I got to take the peace studies class because it led me to people like you two. I think many people in this area are uninformed or just not that knowledgeable about the culture of the Middle East and about the Islamic religion. I personally am interested in Middle East relations, especially after spending three months in Israel last summer.

I want to be an advocate for change and plan to use my power as a strong and independent youth to bring hope for a more peaceful future. I also would love to acknowledge your friendship to one another—it made me smile.

Thank you and good luck,
Miranda Ayres

Dear Amr and Abdallah:

In school, we are taught that America is the best country in the world and that every other country needs our help. Hearing your perspective on American foreign policy helped me to confirm that that is not the case. Hearing about your personal experiences living in Jordan and the United States made me realize that sometimes our "aid" does more harm than good.

Thank you both for taking the time to speak to our class. I hope you have continued success and happiness in your lives.

Sincerely,
Julia Kaplan

Dear Amr and Abdallah:

Our generation tends to be blind to issues outside the US Our media often reports what makes us look good. Thank you so much for coming in to tell us the truth. Islam is thrown in with terrorism and fear, but in reality it is a beautiful and peaceful religion. Both of you accentuated this point very well, and you made some great comparisons. Our foreign policy is invasive and unnecessary. I feel ashamed when I think of all the harm we have done abroad. I found it interesting when you shared that not one of our foreign policy agendas have been fulfilled.

I don't understand how America can't see all the harm we care causing. You mentioned that two million people have died since we invaded in 2003. But we don't hear about those deaths, we just hear about the recent deaths in Paris.

I hope our country takes the initiative to learn more about the issues that surround us. Because if we knew more, maybe we would try to stop it.

Sincerely,
Madison Shaffer

Dear Abdallah and Amr:

Your words were so informative and relevant, especially since the recent massacre in Paris. It is important to get our generation as culturally aware as possible, especially about Islam. Ignorance is the root of most hatred, and we must eliminate as much ignorance as possible.

I learned more and became more aware about Islam and the strong difference (basically no relation at all) between Islam and terrorist groups like ISIS. I'm sure my classmates learned just as much as well.

Keep up the good work. Educate our generation. Lessen the ignorance.

Thank you so much,
Maya Holland

26

AMONG THE BETTER-KNOWN and well-regarded East Coast retreats is the Acorn Commune, a seventy-five-acre farm in rural Louisa County, Virginia, where some thirty members and occasional interns and guests live as a nonviolent, anarchist, secular, income-sharing, egalitarian intentional community. It is self-supporting from its sales of non-GMO heirloom seeds at the Southern Exposure Seed Exchange. Members are expected to work forty hours a week in services that range from raising crops for the communal table to carpentry, baking, and childcare.

One of the recent members is Laura Moore, a peace studies and 2014 B-CC alum.

"I first came to Acorn to do a six-month internship in January 2015," she writes. "I decided to apply for membership in May 2015 and have been a member since. I had been planning to make my internship at Acorn part of a gap year before going to St. Mary's College of Maryland in the fall. However, I began to feel so intertwined in and fulfilled by the project here that I didn't want to leave. Life in the community is more intentional—each day I am entirely self-motivated. I have no boss, no paycheck, and I pay no rent. In community all work is considered equal, including domestic work. So labor creditable activities include things such as cooking a meal, building a barn, and taking care of a sick person. This acknowledgement of the value of domestic work—especially traditionally considered women's work—is a huge reason why I decided to move to community.

"This summer, I was able to visit another community in the FEC (Federation of Egalitarian Communities) called East Wind, in Southern Missouri. I've decided to become a dual member—spending half of my time at Acorn and half at East Wind. Having grown up in the DC area, it's fairly easy for me to get restless in the country. But I think alternating between two such dynamic and driven communities will help keep me from getting too stir-crazy

"My work scene here changes as my desires do. Mostly I do childcare, office work, and events for our heirloom seed business, cleaning and some carpentry. Since I've moved to the community I've learned how to do all kinds of customer service, how to help run a large company's inventory. I've built a stage where parties and performance happen. I've become a better baker, organizer, and communicator, and there's much, much more to learn. My two current educational projects are learning how to weld and how to play the banjo. Since there are so many people of such diverse backgrounds, I have access to knowledge and skills that I wouldn't in the mainstream world—or that I'd have to pay to acquire.

"When I was at B-CC, I felt a very strong pressure to take as many higher-level classes as possible, regardless of my interests in the subjects. I mostly ignored this suggestion, taking as many electives as I could and primarily taking IB classes, which I felt were more flexible and creatively minded than the rigid AP courses. Peace studies was one of my favorite electives. I wish it were a required class for all B-CC students. The competitive, cutthroat culture of Bethesda, and especially B-CC, is not one that fosters compassion. The topics we discussed and the guest speakers regularly pushed me out of the B-CC tunnel vision. I would remember that there was a big, wide world outside of college applications and interpersonal drama. This reminder is helpful not only for escaping the intensity of the school but also for encouraging students to examine the world around them and their participation in it. Which is a big part of why I live where I do. I want to live my activism by putting my time and energy into an egalitarian, consensus-based anarchist and feminist community."

Dear Laura:

Acorn sounds like a paradise. I personally am planning on giving in to societal expectations and going to a fascist, capitalist university, but I have never had my belief of college being the vital next step in our lives shaken until yesterday. You showed us all a life we don't have to live based on what your parents or your society want you to do.

I don't think any of us had ever really thought about alternatives to a formal college education. You lead a truly inspirational life in Virginia, and I hope more people in my class will consider looking to find alternatives to going to college.

Thank you so much for taking some of your time at home to come to us, and I hope your bakery career works out.

Sincerely,
Henry Greenblatt

Dear Laura:

A lot people don't think about their actions or decisions in high school. People, especially at B-CC, live their lives in the grip of expectations. College just seems like the natural choice but in reality it's not.

I admire your ability to step into the unknown. I personally have many reasons for wanting to go to college, but I also see a huge benefit of living in a society like Acorn—a place where you can be outdoors, live with others, and a place where you are released from many aspects of life that stress us out (like income, jealousy of possessions, and expectations).

I really hope I can visit Acorn someday. I feel like it would a place of peace and happiness. I'll be sure to e-mail you!

Thank you so much for your visit.

Sincerely,
Madison Shaffer

Dear Laura:

Your life in the commune sounds peaceful and like a great learning experience. So thank you very much for waking up early to talk to us. Your visit made me reconsider my plans for after high school. We are all on the same path as you are, and I never feel as though it was right for me. I don't think I've had enough experience to want to go right into college next year. I have been looking for a gap-year program that allows me to move somewhere new and learn something valuable.

Thank you for speaking with us and sharing your experiences. I hope you have found something you love to do.

Sincerely,
Lauren Smith

27

T HEY ARE INTENSIVISTS, the physicians in hospitals who spe-
cialize in critical care medicine and who know their way around
nasogastric or endotracheal tubes and hemofiltration equipment for
acute renal failure and where to find the glossopharyngeal cranial nerves.
As the nation's supply of physicians dwindles—losing up to one hundred thousand by 2025, according to a recent report by the Association
of American Medical Colleges report—it appears that critical care medicine itself is in critical condition. If the nation's nonrural hospitals were
adequately staffed with intensive care physicians, fifty-three thousand
lives and $5.4 billion would be saved annually, reports the association.

Another problematic issue was reported on October 11, 2016,
by the Leapfrog Hospital Safety Grade, that well over four hundred
thousand people die annually because of errors made by doctors
and nurses in hospitals. Of the six hospitals in the Washington area,
MedStar Georgetown University Hospital had the second-highest
rating—behind only Sibley Hospital.

A place to find Daniel Jamieson is the ICU at MedStar
Georgetown. His path there included being in the peace studies class
in his senior year at B-CC in 1995. Four years later, he graduated from
Wesleyan University, a school that was the academic home for thir-
ty-two years of Professor Philip Hallie. His enduring books include
Lest Innocent Blood Be Shed, From Cruelty to Goodness, and *Tales of
Good and Evil, Help and Harm.* He died in 1994 at age seventy-two.

After Wesleyan, Daniel earned a medical degree from the Weill
Medical College of Cornell University in 2006, followed by a resi-

dency at the University of Colorado Anschutz Medical campus. In August 2005 he married a Wesleyan classmate, Jennie Rabinowitz, a wedding officiated by Rabbi Renee Feller at the Regis Hotel in Manhattan. During his talk to the peace studies class Daniel spoke easily of his good fortune in marrying Jennie, which prompted several students to invite her to speak.

Daniel also spoke of his parents, his mother a social worker and father a lawyer, as well as his sister Katherine who was a peace studies student at B-CC and went on to become a writer after serving in the Peace Corps in Guyana.

After Daniel's conversation with the class, few students left without deep feelings of admiration for both his work as an ICU physician and being a med-school professor whose duties included interviewing students applying to Georgetown.

> Dear Dr. Jamieson:
>
> Ever since I was a kid, I've wanted to be a surgeon. My bookshelves are filled with anatomy books, medical journals, and my very own suture kit. I couldn't tell you exactly what made me want to pursue medicine. Maybe it was the forever expanding field of science, maybe it was the opportunity to save lives—or it was people like you. Becoming a doctor takes an immense amount of dedication and passion.
>
> Thank you so much for coming to our class. I intern every afternoon at Walter Reed National Medical Center in the neurosurgery department, but the doctors never have time to talk to me.
>
> I really appreciate your taking time to explain your career and your journey to where you are now. Maybe one day you'll be interviewing me.
>
> Thank you again!
>
> Sincerely,
> Madison Shaffer

Dear Dr. Dan:

Thank you for coming back to the greatest school in the land. It is really uplifting to hear former Barons speak about their time here at B-CC and how their experiences changed them to what they are today. It was fascinating how you want to save lives and how you want to see a change in the processes of giving care to patients.

My little sister wishes to be a doctor someday, and I bet that she would love to hear from you. I do not know if you are a believer or not, but God has truly blessed you with a career that not all can do. I wish that future doctors and doctors of today will have the passion as you. Maybe more people will be saved than those who die from preventable mistakes by doctors who just do it as part of the business. Sometimes I wondered if my uncle's and cousin's deaths could have been prevented.

Sincerely,
Derrick Jones

Dear Dr. Dan:

I was delighted when I heard you would be our guest speaker because I have been strongly considering a career in neurobiology, medicine, or health science, and I was excited to hear about what it's like to be a doctor. It's challenging for me to find opportunities to hear firsthand about the experiences of people who work in medicine. You provided me with a lot of insight into the field.

Thank you for explaining why you became a doctor and what you like and dislike about working in critical care. Your visit to our class has reinforced my desire to have a career that helps

people on a personal level, that makes a difference in society and that I enjoy—whether that
ends up being health-related or something else.

I imagine you have a pretty busy schedule,
and I greatly appreciate that you were able to
spend time to talk with us.

Sincerely,
Sarah Mayhew

Dear Dr. Dan:

I could never be a doctor, especially in the
unit you work in, dealing with people who are on
death's doorstep. What you do is incredible, caring for people in their most vulnerable and needy
state. Personally I wouldn't have the courage to
take the reins of someone else's life or the strength
to steer them to recovery. I would have a similar
reaction that you mentioned you have with sick
children: I would be too horrified to act. One of
my greatest fears is to fall ill like the people you
take care of. Working with them would undoubt-
edly give me stress and anxiety beyond belief.

I am just so glad and grateful that people
like you have the bravery to do what I could
never do myself.

Thank you for visiting our class, and more
importantly, thank you for dedicating your life to
the lives of others.

Sincerely and gratefully,
Conor Smyth

Dear Dan:

As you may know, it's the time of year
when seniors are applying to college. It's been

pretty stressful so far because where we decide to go now will decide what path we go down. It's uplifting to see B-CC alums who come back and say they've made it. Your story about your high school dance helped me understand that things that happen in high school will *not* stick with your forever.

I've always been interested in being a nurse, although after shadowing my aunt at the hospital where she works, I can say it's not for me.

We are grateful to have you come to our class, and thank you for saving the lives of so many.

Olivia Goodman

Dear Dr. Dan:

I am really thankful to have been able to talk to an ICU doctor outside of the hospital. I am someone who is interested in medicine and someone who has been in a hospital bed many times. I found it eye-opening to see the other perspective. I understand why you don't work in pediatrics. When I stayed in the emergency room at Children's overnight, I heard a child code three times. It was really painful to see that, and I can't imagine seeing it every day.

I want to thank you for coming to our class, but more than that would like to thank you for doing a job many could not. I hope to one day help others as you do, and I hope to have the strength to let learn to let go when it is time.

Thank you,
Dani Seltzer

28

C ONGRESS WAS HAVING one of its better days in 1789 when it proposed the Sixth Amendment to the Constitution that "in all criminal prosecutions the accused shall enjoy... the assistance of counsel for his defense."

Well said, Founders, but what if you are among the broke and broken who have no money to pay a lawyer? It wasn't until Gideon v Wainright, a 1963 case in which the Supreme Court ruled that the penniless indigent charged with a crime had a right to a lawyer paid by the state. Gideon was the gateway decision that led to public defender agencies throughout the countries. The ranks of public defender lawyers range from the skilled and idealistic who have little taste for corporate law and $900 billable hour cases to those who scrape along on the margins of jurisprudence.

Jennie Rabinowitz belongs to the former. She graduated from Great Neck North High School on Long Island in 1995 and Wesleyan University in 1999 where she met Dan Jamieson who she married in 2005 a year before she earned her JD from Yeshiva University's Cardozo School of Law. The next four years found her in Denver using her professional gifts to stand with impoverished clients that many would dismiss as society's debris.

"It may not seem that long," Jennie writes of her public defender practice in Denver,

"but it was enough time to go from handling misdemeanors to all manner of felony cases, including homicides and sexual assault cases. My clients were people who were facing criminal charges who could not afford to hire private counsel. Some were innocent, some were guilty. I believe that every person should be judged on more than their own worst moments, and so I never had a problem advocating for my clients. My most challenging cases involved children who were being prosecuted as adults. They were housed in adult jails where they were often kept in solitary confinement, ostensibly for their own safety. At the time there was nothing that defense attorneys or judges could do about it, since decisions fell exclusively to prosecutors. These children were often terrified, confused, and mentally fragile. Their stays in solitary sometimes ended in suicide."

"It was heartbreaking. Spending my free time outdoors and in nature—as far away from jail or prison as I could go—helped me cope with the intense pressure of my work and kept me energized. After I had my son my caseload and the emotional weight of my clients' hardships combined with parental duties left me in a constant state of exhaustion. I no longer felt that my judgment was solid, and I felt like I was failing as both an advocate and as a parent. I decided to leave my practice, at least for the time being. I miss the joy of fighting for social justice every day, and the satisfaction I got from standing up for people who no one else would stand up for. I hope that I can raise my children to value all human life and to work for a just world."

Dear Ms. Jennie:

Wow! Your story gave me chills as you talked about 9/11, how families of undocumented immigrants felt as those loved ones disappeared. I got goose bumps. I admire the heart you have as always seeing good in every single person. I don't know if you believe in God, but as a Christian, you are one incredible human that I believe God sent as a gift to this world.

I wish you nothing but the best for you and your family. Thank you for having an inner light and letting it shine through this dark world.

Michelle

Dear Jennie:

People often lose perspective on the integrity and humanity that exists in the world of law and tend to see it as a profession filled with "crooks" and "scam artists." So hearing about your genuine care for clients and persistent work in your field was very refreshing.

I still question how lawyers are so often able to defend obviously guilty people, even though they claim they're just "doing their job," but your perspective has caused me to view it under a different light.

Thank you,
Sebastian Langan

Dear Jennie:

Throughout your time here, I literally could not take my eyes and ears off your story. I found it extremely interesting and wonderfully captivating. Thank you so much for speaking. It made me feel better about not knowing what I want to be "when I grow up." I hope that whatever I end up doing, I can do it with as much passion and dedication as you. I also believe that there is good in every person and that we all just need to try harder to recognize the good we all share.

Best luck,
Miranda Ayres

29

IN 1973, WHEN she was eleven, Courtney Freeman discovered Transcendental Meditation. She recalls, "My dad was a very liberal professor at George Mason University who one day packed us up in the family station wagon and took us to a TM Center in Washington where we all received our mantra. My mom and sister did not take to it much, but my dad and I began to practice regularly. I found a deep sense of calm and wholeness from my meditation, even from a young age. As a teenager, my regular practice was crowded out by an early a.m. paper route and after-school sports and homework. At one point in during my junior year in high school, my father determined that I was getting a little bratty. His solution was to send me away for a weekend meditation retreat. I loved it!"

Socializing with other meditators, Courtney met "people who told me about the Maharishi International University in Fairfield Iowa where all the students and faculty practice TM. My plans for college had included applying to the local schools—University of Virginia, Madison, and Virginia Tech—but I secretly felt a pang of knowingness that perhaps MIU might be the right place for me."

Courtney hied off to Iowa and the Fairfield campus. She was enamored but not totally. Still shopping, she took a look at UVA. A friend showed her around the campus, saying, "I really want you to show you something." They went upstairs to a dorm that had a common room that was decorated on walls from ceiling to floor with empty alcohol bottles: vodka, run, gin, you name it. "I did say 'wow' when I saw this as it did look pretty cool. But inside I thought to myself, *I don't think this is something to be proud of.* My priorities are different from these students. I have done my share of partying, but I wanted to move more toward my developing my consciousness through pure and healthy ways. That's it, decision made. I'm going to MIU."

Two of Courtney's daughters, Katherine and Brigitte, were in the peace studies classes. Both were models of graciousness. Katherine, now a senior at the University of Vermont, is a year away from medical school and Brigitte is at the University of Delaware.

Dear Ms. Freeman:

It was good fun to see you in our class. You spoke so well, and you were engaging, which is hard to do for an early morning class. I've always admired you and your family's dedication to meditation. I remember when I was younger I used to come over to see you guys and you would be upstairs meditating. I also remember once you tried to tech me how. My mind is too hectic to meditate, but I tried my best.

I agree with everything you said. I think if we all took time to find peace within ourselves then the world would be a calmer and less violent place.

Thank you for coming in to talk with us. Maybe I'll try meditating again!

Sincerely,
Madison Shaffer

Dear Ms. Freeman:

I 100 percent agree with your theory about an anger epidemic in this country. It is a real problem, and I am glad someone is trying to expose it. The work you do with TM and mindfulness is undervalued and so incredibly important to our society. Maybe if Donald Trump meditated more, he wouldn't be such a god-awful person.

This kind of work will change the world. Thank you so much for taking the time out of your day to speak to us.

Sincerely,
Henry Greenblatt

Dear Mrs. Freeman:

I agree with you that TM has medical benefits and that I should try to practice it more frequently. Unfortunately, I tend to forget to attempt it when I have time on my hands. I think it's wonderful that you've raised your children with a more relaxed and open mind frame because of regular meditation. I really think this is something more people should take to. As you said, a more peaceful nation must spring from more peaceful families.

Thank you,
Sebastian Langan

Dear Mrs. Freeman:

I have never really tried to mediate before until you came to speak to our class. After meditating with you, I felt more awake and relaxed. Now I know that meditating makes me more relaxed.

Thank for coming to our class, and I hope you continue to have happiness and success in your life.

Sincerely,
Julia Kaplan

30

ENROLLING AT THE University of Maryland in the mid-1980s, Tim Wessel planned to become a pediatric dentist. Among the science requirements was an introductory course in horticulture. As someone who "always loved the outdoors and working with my hands," Tim began thinking that opening the mouths of children was becoming less attractive than one day opening his own landscaping company. It happened on April 2, 1989, calling his company Timothy's Garden. He learned the game after summering in jobs ranging from gardening at a private club to being a salesman for a design company specializing in landscaping.

"I had a small client list and grew from there," he recalls about the early days. "It is difficult to sum up self-employment but I have to say that I really feel fortunate to be my own boss, even though I have over a hundred 'bosses' [clients] that I answer to. My schedule has allowed me to take part in my children's activities all through their childhoods—very important to me. I have relationships with clients who trust me and allow me to work. I love the landscape business—a great meld of art *and* science."

Conscientious, Tim Wessel is well aware of the negatives in working the land. "I know, like any business, my actions affect the environment. My trucks and machines spew fumes. I do my best to minimize my carbon footprint. One rationalization that I tell myself is that the thousands of trees and plants will live on and maybe neutralize the pollution that I have caused."

Then there are the pesticides: "I use as little of them as possible. I've lost some clients over my underuse of pesticides and what they consider unsatisfactory results. The creation of man-made gardens goes against nature, which will do its best to keep a space natural. We, man, have invented all kinds of ways to keep nature at bay. Some good, many bad. Gardens can be beautiful works of art to enjoy visually and even better, to enjoy physically. We must do our best to use methods of design, installation, and maintenance that strike a balance with nature. As a landscaper, I need to educate my clients on appropriate actions that are better for the garden, the clients, and their kids and the environment. I try. It is a challenge. I love plants, the outdoors, and people."

Let's add the students at B-CC. Among them is Tim's daughter, a member of the spring peace studies semester and who is on her way to the University of Maryland.

> Hey, Dad!
>
> Even with the last-minute notice, you still managed to come to class and kill it with your presentation. Thank you for taking the time out of your busy schedule to show everyone how incredible of a dad, businessman, and husband you are. Even I learned something new.
>
> Your passion is inspiring, and I know that you really made an impact on the class.
>
> Love you!
>
> Lillian

> Dear Tim Wessel:
>
> Few things are more admirable than starting a business from the ground up. Along with your accomplishments, I was amazed and inspired by your presentation and motivational speech. I'm not the biggest risk-taker in the world. Or

"wasn't." I know where I want to go in life, and you've inspired me to jump through those hoops and persevere. Thank you!

Sariya Ismail

PS: That egg trick was awesome.*
*Without doubt. The awesomeness is all but beyond description involving a half dozen eggs, a broom, and compression—with the trick being successful when eggs do not break. None did in either of the two classes.

Dear Mr. Tim:

After taking environmental science this year, I have become interested in agriculture and sustainability. I think it is impressive that you were able to start your own business and pursue what you love. I also appreciate your attempt to use fewer pesticides when gardening. There is definitely an overuse of chemicals, especially when it comes to food production. I wish you the best in your future business plans and thank you for talking to our class.

Sincerely,
Jenna Troccoli

PS: I loved your egg trick.

Dear Mr. Tim:

I am going into the arts, and I am always worried I won't succeed, but when I hear people share their stories about jobs that are not traditional, it gives me hope that I'll be okay. You inspired me to do my best and to really follow my heart.

Sincerely,
Sonia Picard

PS: I love Lillian and will probably see you soon.

Dear Mr. Tim:

The bathroom must be your favorite room in your house with all the water you drank during your talk. Your presentation was really inspirational when it comes to doing what you want and doing it successfully. Your jokes were funny and kept me focused. I also loved the story of how you met your wife, and it is so good you guys are still together. It gives me hope leaving high school that I will keep in touch with my friends.

There is so much ahead of us and your speech helped me think about the future in a less stressful way.

Your egg demonstration was funny and yet inspirational.

Thank you,
Cindy Pontachack

Dear Mr. Wessel:

Congratulations on your successful trick! We were left guessing what the cups and eggs were for and then even after you set it up and what was going to happen. Regardless, your talk was terrific. After taking AP environmental science last year, it was awesome to be able to understand all your insight into IPM and pesticide usage. It was also fascinating to hear the business end of things which is something I'm considering studying in college. Thank you again for a wonderful and entertaining talk!

Katie Weber

31

I N 1959 WHEN the Dalai Lama fled from Tibet to India, Thupten Phelgye was three. To avoid the brutalities of the Chinese invaders, he was hidden in a barn by his parents. They would soon spend twenty-four days crossing the Himalayas to India, there to live in a refugee camp. After working washing dishes and clothes, he ran away at age thirteen to join the Tibetan military in 1969, in hateful anger at the Chinese. He was not accepted and returned to attend school. In 1972, His Holiness the Dalai Lama came to speak of kindness and compassion. "I took a U-turn," Thupten Phelgye recalls, one that led him at seventeen to enter the Sera Jey Buddhist monastery in South India as a novice. In 1991, after eighteen years of Buddhist studies, he earned a Geshe degree, akin to a PhD. Going deeper, he would devote five years at a retreat in the Himalayas, being guided by the Dalai Lama. In 1997 he founded the Universal Compassion Foundation, a nonprofit specializing in vegetarianism, cruelty-free diets, and animal rights. In recent years he has been on the faculty of Eastern Washington University in Spokane. Geshe Phelgye was brought to B-CC by his stouthearted friend Annie Mahon.

"I am a vegetarian," he told the students whose eyes opened wide at the sight of the holy man's flowing scarlet-and-gold robes, "because I want to cause as little harm as possible as I go through this life. I try to cause less pain, less suffering. Life is precious for all living beings. As much as possible, do no harm. It's a choice between harming and not harming."

Dear Venerable Geshe Phelgye:

It was truly an honor to have the opportunity to meet you and listen to your story yesterday. It is amazing that you made it out of Tibet alive and were able to turn your life around and make a positive out of a negative. Your work with animal rights activism is inspiring as well. You are a blessing to this world.

Thank you so much for visiting our class. I hope you will stop by the Kunzang Palyul Choling Temple in Poolesville, Maryland, at some point in the future.

Sincerely,
Elizabeth Mulvihill (Buddhist Girl)
Om mani pad me hung!

Dear Geshe Thupten Phelgye:

I greatly appreciate the presentation you gave our class and the insights to the life of Tibetan refugee. I as well as many others were unaware of the details of China's takeover of Tibet, and I feel I have learned in a way that our educational system is unable to teach.

Your ideals of a meat-free diet and support of animal rights resonated with me. I believe as well that to create a peaceful society, the meat industry must come to an end.

Thank you for all that you've given our class as well as the change you've sparked in the world.

Sincerely,
Sydney Jesus-Allen

Dear Geshe:

I think Buddhism is one of the most fascinating religions there are. I grew up in Thailand in a household where my parents would tell me stories about monks.

I would also like to be an animal rights activist since I'm planning on becoming a vet in the future. I've loved animals for as long as I can remember, and being a vet has been my passion.

Thank you so much for enlightening us on your life and your beliefs. I think it's amazing.

Best regards,
Maria Villegas

Dear Geshe:

You live a life I have not encountered in my own. In a country that glorifies violence and runs on the stress of people trying to achieve the "American Dream," your outlook on life was refreshing. I want to thank you for coming to our class to share your beliefs and insights. Your journey to get where you are now is unconventional but gives me hope that I will have the strength to separate from the masses without fear. I hope someday to achieve the level of peace and happiness you have reached.
I wish you all the best,

Sincerely,
Dani Seltzer

Dear Mr. Geshe:

I am seeing the world differently after being touched by your experiences. You helped me realize that First World problems are not real problems. I should not be upset that my phone is broken or my debit card is out of money when there is so much you worked for in your childhood.

You have inspired me to appreciate life more.

Love,
Aniqa Ahmed

Dear Professor Geshe Phelgye:

Your visit was on a topic most dear to my heart: kindness. Through the course of my high school education I have learned more and more about this world, and each new discovery is a blessing. My favorite story, and I think yours as well, was my conversion to veganism, which sheds light on the many hidden acts of violence toward animals that go unnoticed.

I regret not being able to attend your panel discussion last evening [at the Quaker Meeting House on Florida Avenue in Washington], but I hope there was the same awakening and conversion for those who were there as you and I experienced.

Thank you for your gentle thoughts and words.

Sincerely,
Liza Brilliant

Dear Dr. Geshe Thupten Phelgye:

It was great to see your smile in our classroom. It was incredibly eye-opening to hear your story and see the grace and peace in the way you've handled it. I think it's impressive how you've been a vegetarian for so long and stick to your ethical stance on that issue.

I love how you emphasized logic and reasoning as a major player in your morality. Also, it really made my day that you were so smiley and happy when you were talking.

I'd love to understand more about Buddhist philosophy, like the proof of reincarnation. What you said made a lot of sense to me, and the values you mentioned really sat well with my conscience.

Thank you for coming. I hope to see you soon again.

Natalie Tomeh

Dear Geshe:

I was so inspired after hearing your story. I really appreciate your coming to share it with us. As another vegetarian who made my conversion similar to yours, I felt a connection to what you were saying. I also l loved to learn that you have been working to promote peace in the Middle East. I work with an organization in Israel that does the same. It brings together Israeli, Jewish, Palestinian, Muslim, and Christian teenagers to break down stigmas and promote cooperation. I love the values that you stand for and represent.

I appreciate your coming to share them.

Sincerely,
Celia Goldfarb

32

"ALL HAPPY FAMILIES are alike," wrote Leo Tolstoy in the opening line of *Anna Karenina*, while "each unhappy family is unhappy in its own way."

If more families roused themselves to act on the advice of Aviva Goldfarb to regularly come together for dinner, their Tolstoyan happiness could be assured. But with many children pressured by their overscheduled lives while their overworked parents may not leave the office or workplace until seven or eight, family dinners can be rare.

"Like many busy moms," Aviva says, "I initially struggled to put a nutritious dinner on the table for my family amid the chaos of daily life. Recalling my own mom's simple weekly mean planning strategy, I developed a system that helps parents take the 'Scramble' out of the dinner hour by giving them an easy, online meal planning and grocery shopping system, along with failproof family-friendly recipes."

The system became The Six O'Clock Scramble, a company Aviva founded in 2006 that works with families to take time for dinner and embrace the benefits of mealtime socializing. Her four books include *The Six O'Clock Scramble: Quick, Healthy, and Delicious Dinner Recipes for Busy Families.* She has written for *The Washington Post, USA Today, O Magazine* and appears on NBC's *Today Show*.

Aviva, whose daughter Celia is in the peace studies class, graduated from Santa Barbara High School in 1986 and the University of Pennsylvania in 1990. Marrying in 1994, her husband Andrew is an attorney specializing in litigation. The November 4 *Washington Post* carried a heartfelt article by Aviva titled "Savoring Our Last Year of Family Dinners." With her son Solomon already in college, Aviva wrote: "With Celia's impending departure for college—although still nine months away—I have been steeling myself to face weekday dinners with neither of our children at the table. For any parent, that prospect is daunting."

> Dear Mrs. Goldfarb:
>
> In my family we have dinner a couple of times a month. Given that it happens so infrequently, it's definitely not something that I take for granted. When we do all sit down, it's usually me who cooks and finds a time when everyone is available. I haven't focused on trying to do this as much recently, but after hearing you speak I think I will try to organize a family dinner again soon.
>
> You helped me understand the importance of eating together. You also gave several good reasons to eat organically grown and ethically raised food from local farms.
>
> I am impressed that you and your family eat together so often, and that you are so passionate about this practice that you run a business to make it work for other families. I plan to subscribe to your YouTube channel —and maybe I'll try to make those pumpkin enchiladas you mentioned.
>
> Thank you sincerely,
> Sarah Mayhew

> Dear Mrs. Goldfarb:
>
> Thanks for taking time out of your daily routine to talk with us about the importance of a family eating healthy meals together at dinner-

time and how these family values and traditions relate to the lessons in peace studies.

My family has never eaten at the dinner table since I was a child. When I get home from whatever I was doing like school or football practice they would ask me how it was, and then I would say "it was fine." Then I would walk away. For me, I'm not much of a talker, though some would say I talk too much. They say that because they see me as annoying on what I like to talk about.

It is funny how when my mom makes a big Thanksgiving dinner, we all fill our plates and then go to our rooms or back to the TV and watch the Thanksgiving football games.

I hope that my very own family will eat at dinner together every night so that my children will know how to be connected to others naturally, instead of being connected to others at the touch of your fingertips with the technology of today everyday of their lives.

Sincerely,
Derrick Jones

Dear Mrs. Goldfarb:

While I don't always want to eat dinner with my family, whether from annoyance with my brothers, aggravation with my parents, or simply a large workload I need to complete, I certainly understand and respect family dinner's merits. What you told us about how kids in families that eat dinner together more often, even when controlled for other variable, experience less stress and tension, it did not surprise me. I think what you are doing—writing cookbooks and setting up meal plans for families—contributes a great deal more to communities than one might expect at first glance.

Many people are far too rushed to be able to come up with and cook a meal for their family on their own. So the services you provide with *The Six O'Clock Scramble* save time, money, and energy. Not only that, having meals ready and having family dinners allows everyone to have to worry about one less thing and give them an opportunity to express themselves and make stronger social connections. When families share their feelings with one another, they can settle interpersonal as well as intrapersonal conflicts more easy instead of letting their feelings get bottled up inside, building up over time and erupting in a single outburst.

Thank you for taking time to visit our class.

Sincerely,
Conor Smythe

Dear Mrs. Goldfarb:

Your story was so inspiring to me—to see someone who had one idea for her life but then taking an entirely different path. And being successful too. Truly amazing.

Thank you so much for showing me that I succeed in any profession I choose.

Just so you know, my family eats dinner together quite often—although we may not be as harmonious as you and your family are.

Thank you for visiting! You're awesome!

Sincerely,
Kate Strathman

Dear Mom:

I love you! I am so lucky to have a mother who has taught me that I can make a living doing what I love. Thank you for all you have done for me. Even though I don't say it enough, I don't take it for granted.

Love,
Celia

33

WITH MUCH OF the public's regard for the media at all-time lows, it's worth taking a moment to appreciate a journalist of proven conscience: Daniella Zalcman. A graduate of Holton-Arms School in Bethesda, Maryland, and who earned a degree from Columbia University in 2009, her father is a psychiatrist with Jewish roots. Her attorney mother is from Vietnam and who became a lawyer. She and her family lived in a home a mile from the Potomac River on land that was once home to the Algonquian Nation. While at Columbia, Daniella won an internship at *The New Yorker* magazine, perhaps thinking that sometime soon it would publish one of her photographs. Which it did. In addition, her documentary photography has appeared in *The New York Times, Vanity Fair, The Wall Street Journal,* and *TIME.*

With grants from the Pulitzer Center for Crisis Reporting, Daniella's major achievement is her 2016 book *Signs of Your Identity.* Referring to the Indian Act of 1876, she writes, "For 120 years the Canadian government operated a network of Indian Residential Schools that were meant to assimilate young indigenous students into the western Canadian culture. Indians agents would take children from their homes as young as two or three and send them to church-run boarding schools where they were punished for speaking their native languages or observing an indigenous traditions, routinely sexually and physically assaulted, and in some extreme instances subjected to medical experimentation and sterilization. The last residential school closed in 1996. The Canadian government issued its first formal apology in 2008."

Daniella traveled to the Treaty Four territory in Saskatchewan, there to dig in with her cameras and notebooks to get the stories of the boarding school survivors. Among them was Marlene McNab, a mental health therapist in Regina, Saskatchewan, who met Daniella in the summer of 2015. "For many years," she writes, "I lived in the dark, in a reactionary state where I ran from my 'triggers' and used drugs and alcohol to medicate my pain and suffering. I didn't know it at the time but I had repressed a lot of traumatic memories and instances of extreme sexual and emotional abuse suffered in residential school… These schools emerged across Canada in waves that became breeding grounds for sickness and all forms of human rights violations."

In the afterword, Daniella writes that her book's genesis "is rooted in my own shame that this version of history as excluded from my textbooks. Indigenous narratives remain a footnote in western education. What little is shared has been flattened and whitewashed. There is a deliberate forgetting of the legacies of colonialism and the effects of intergenerational trauma. I hope that, in some small way, I can help correct that."

> Dear Daniella:
>
> I am astonished at the lack of coverage of Native American history in our school's curriculum. I wish I were able to learn about the struggles imposed on indigenous peoples. I appreciate the overview you gave our class.
>
> I can't imagine how much more there is to learn, but it was a great kick-start to my interest and awareness of these abuses. Your double-exposure photographs you showed us were stunning and moving. I was especially surprised when you told us about the treatment of the Indian residential school students and that they were stripped

of their culture and prohibited from speaking in their native tongue.

Your presentation changed my perspective, made me appreciate the privileges I have, and led me to question the practices of our school systems. I hope to find more opportunities to gain information about residential schools and the tribal nations.

Thank you for the important work you do in bringing awareness to this underacknowledged issue in a creative and touching way. Thank you for sharing it with our class.

Most sincerely,
Sarah Mayhew

Dear Daniella:

I was shocked and appalled to realize that such atrocities were committed against native people both here and in Canada, yet we are too concerned with our American pride to take responsibility for these violent actions. It is possible that without you here to enlighten us we never would have had a way to realize this had happened. In the future, I will be doing more research and educating those around me, so they can become aware of this also.

Thank you for reporting this. I look forward to seeing your work in the future. And I'm sure I will.

Sincerely,
Celia Goldfarb

Dear Daniella:

Your work is truly amazing, and believe me, it is important. These schools, stories, and people are not written about in our history books, so how can we learn about them without people like you. They say a picture tells a thousand words but yours tell a full story—one that has been swept under the carpet of shame and embarrassment. These residential schools are among the most disgraceful institutions. It is unbelievable that we continue to oppress our First Nation people with vicious stereotypes and excluding their stories and ancestors from our history.

I wish for you to continue your work: for the young people whose eyes you have opened and hearts you have touched, like my own.

Many thanks to you and your friends at the Pulitzer Center.

Sincerely
Liza Brilliant

34

COURAGE COMES IN varicolored forms. It isn't especially common in high school which explains why Marxe Orbach has large numbers of admirers at B-CC. Suffering from depression, which often left the sixteen-year-old struggling to rise from bed to walk to school, Marxe's psychiatrist advised he acquire a service dog. He did: a curly-haired black poodle that Marxe named Truffle Bear.

The Americans With Disabilities Act defines a service animal as "any dog that is individually trained to do work or perform tasks for the benefit of an individual with a disability, including physical, sensory, psychiatric, intellectual or other mental disabilities." Truffle Bear had been trained to go further and be an emotional service dog that according to the ADA can provide "companionship, relieve loneliness and sometimes help with depression, anxiety and certain phobias."

In early 2016 Marxe, supported by those close to him, revealed that he is transgender. The pressure of that, plus the sudden passing of his father, led to a hospitalization. It was then that his psychiatrist recommended a service dog.

For the first few weeks of the school year, school administrators welcomed Truffle Bear into the hallways and classrooms. Then, as reported by Bethesda magazine, the pup "was kicked out" due to "acting unruly during yoga class." Questions arose whether the school system's regulations for service animals were being met. After being forced to stay home for a week, which deepened Marxe's depression, the issue of behavior was resolved. That it took a week didn't speak especially well for the B-CC administration.

I came to know Marxe during his first year at B-CC. He wanted to enroll in my class but was told that it was only for seniors. I asked the school's guidance counselors to make an exception for Marxe, a request that, sadly, was denied. The next year, I invited him to come tell his story to my two classes. He heart-connected with every student.

Dear Marxe:

Your visit to our class yesterday gave me some insight into an issue I had never thought much about before: mental health issues and, specifically, treatment of those with mental illnesses. It's amazing what you have gone through just over the past couple of weeks, what with your dispute with the administration over being allowed to bring a service dog with you to school.

Obviously, having Truffle Bear here with you helps you a lot. I don't think the administration had any credible claim to taking him away, especially since you've already had him with you at school for almost a month. I'm glad you won that battle, and I wish you luck in any future disputes. I have no doubt Truffle Bear will continue to provide you great happiness and support.

Sincerely,
Conor Smyth

Dear Marxe:

I was so inspired by hearing about your journey. I know it wasn't easy to talk about personal and sensitive issues like mental health, and I am grateful for your willingness in doing so. I am impressed your resilience and perseverance in coming to school with a smile even after all the difficulty they imposed on you.

While I don't know exactly what you've had to go through, I understand how difficult it can be just to get through the day, especially with mental illness taking its toll. It truly is an illness. I am happy that you are finding ways to cope that work best for you.

Seeing you and Truffle Bear in the halls always brightens my day, not only because *I love* dogs but also because it makes me happy to know that he provides support for you.

Thank you for so much for sharing your story! I hope you have a great year, and good luck on catching up on any work you missed during your time off school.

Sarah

Dear Marxe:

Thank you for showing our class a different side of B-CC. Many people pass you in the hall and don't know much about your story. I don't want to speak for others, but I know you've inspired me. I've struggled with my own sense of identity in the LGBTQ community as well my mental illness, and seeing you improve gives me hope. I know it's different for every person, but I know what it's like to be debilitated by mental illness. Hearing your story was truly inspiring. Feel free to contact me anytime. I'd love to talk more.

Sincerely,
Sydney Jesus-Allen

Dear Marxe:

I think you are fantastic. I know you've been through so much, but you're resilient and strong, and we're lucky to have heard you speak. I'm thrilled that you and your family were able to fight back against the school as they tried to take Truffle Bear away, because I, as well as so many others, love seeing him the hallways. Keep staying strong and keep being you.

Sincerely,
Celia Goldfarb

Dear Marxe:

I was so excited to see you and Truffle Bear when I walked into class. I had seen both of you around school but never had the opportunity to say hello and ask the questions that I have. After your visit to the class, I now know that you are the most amazing pair. Both of you help each other in ways that are so living and so necessary.

I am happy when I see you two in the hallway because I know that you are inspiring others to address mental health and to seek treatments that suit their needs.

I hope you have a great year and great future with Truffle Bear.

Sincerely,
Maeve Hennessey

35

W HETHER ON THE north sidewalk of East-West Highway or at the top of the stairs of the main doorway entrance, Tamara Tisdale is a cheerful greeter to students as they pour in for their morning classes. She's a Montgomery County police officer, a seasoned twenty-year veteran who graduated from Howard University in 1994 with a biology major and then earning a master's degree in biology at the University of Maryland in 2001. "Most of my time at B-CC," she says of her four years at the school, "deals with positive interactions. There are times where I am required to handle criminal matters and make arrests. That's the least favorite part of my job."

Her talks to the peace studies classes cover a range of topics: police body cameras, how to carry yourself when pulled over by an officer, police brutality, racial profiling, citizens rights to refuse a breathalyzer test, teenage drinking, texting while driving. Easygoing and engaging, Officer Tisdale is agile in how to relate to students: talk with them, not at them. She was receptive to their stories of dealing with the police—some positive accounts, some negative. She lives in Prince Georges County and is the mother of two, both now in their twenties.

Dear Officer Tisdale:

Over the past few years, the coverage of police malpractice and brutality has overflowed in the mainstream media. It has taken over the news with much the same force as Islamic terrorism.

For this reason, I am skeptical. It didn't surprise me at all when you said that instances of police killings and mistreatment of suspects have not increased (I think they have actually decreased). However, I still think there is a large issue with police brutality and systemic racism in America.

We have a problem when a black person is killed every two days by the police and when, while blacks and whites use marijuana at the roughly the same rate, an overwhelming number of blacks are arrested compared with whites.

For that reason, I think it is important that we have more local officers like you, people who are clearly educated, know what they're doing and know when to restrain themselves when it comes to force. Thank you so much for coming to our class Sincerely,

Conor Smyth

Dear Officer Tisdale:

I would you tell you that I really liked your talk, but I think a better term for it would be a discussion, which I greatly enjoyed. I appreciate how you approached your visit to our class as a conversation. It gave students the opportunity to ask about specific issues and concerns they were curious about.

It was beneficial for me to receive firsthand information and law enforcement policy and personal stories and experiences from a police officer such as yourself.

Thank you for everything you do to protect out school and community. From your visit, I feel as though I will be able to better consider my actions when interacting with the police because I will be more knowledgeable and better able to empathize with them.

Thank you sincerely,
Sarah Mayhew

Dear Officer Tisdale:

As someone who sees herself in law enforcement in the future, I really appreciated hearing your perspective. I never thought of how the cameras of police officers only record the bad things that happen, not the good. I was overjoyed to hear from someone who wanted to work in the field and in the lab. I want to be that person when I am older, one who can investigate crimes while having a scientific outlook

It is uplifting to hear that it is possible and not completely crazy. Thank you for your service. I hope to continue your legacy.

Sincerely,
Dani Seltzer

Dear Officer Tisdale:

I have never had an interaction with a police officer before, so I never really knew the extent of an officer's job. I admire you for the work you that you do. I am grateful for having you at the school to help keep us safe.

I am sorry that the media lately have been portraying police work in a negative light. What we see in the media is not the full story. Thank you for having a strong sense of judgment. I really appreciate your coming in to show us the importance of police officers because I am able to see them in a different light now.

Thank you,
Ilana

36

AMONG DENMARK'S JOURNALISTS, fewer are more appreciated for their honest and singular reporting than Lisbeth Carlsen. On the issues that matter—social justice, education, human rights, criminal justice—she has done it. A 1991 graduate of the Danish School of Journalism in Arhus, Denmark, she won a Fulbright Fellowship that led to earning a master's degree from George Washington University in 1995. Lisbeth, fluent in English, Swedish, and German as well as her native Danish, spoke to the B-CC classes about the invasion of Denmark on April 9, 1940, by Hitler's army. The students prepared for Lisbeth's visit by watching the documentary *A Force More Powerful* that detailed the nonviolent resistance by the Danish people to the Nazi killing machine. In a book of the same name, Peter Ackerman and Jack Duval report that the populace's defiance of the German occupation ranged from work stoppages and strikes to nonviolent sabotage. Heroically it also included coming together to protect Denmark's eight thousand Jews. "With every boatload of Jewish refugees that sailed to Sweden, the Danish resistance could savor another success and each one helped to strengthen the resolve and swell its ranks. Although German soldiers continued to pursue Danish Jews... their efforts were largely in vain as 7, 220 Jews successfully escaped to Sweden. Only 472 were captured... The national solidarity that made the [rescue] operation possible brought Denmark into harder opposition to the Germans and it proved to both the Allies and skeptical Danes that a well-organized resistance effort with tangible, realistic goals could subvert the power of the Third Reich."

Lisbeth Carlsen recalls that "in my family there was one issue that could not be spoken off, not even mentioned with one word." And that was how her elder relatives were terrified and mistreated. "It had to do with my uncle who had been a policeman in Copenhagen during the war. As a little girl, my mother told me that Uncle Gunnar could not speak to anything related to his past as a policeman. He had been to Buchenwald. That was all she said but back then [1970] even kids new what Buchenwald was."

Because the German military feared that if the Allied forces intervened in Denmark, the country's police would join them. As a result, Lisbeth says, on September 19, 1944, "thousands of Danish policemen were lured into coming to work—they faked warnings of an air raid that was not in progress, and when these two thousand men met at their stations, they were captured by German soldiers and forced onto cattle trucks and taken by boat to the death camps. As Danes they were treated far better than the Russians, Jews, and homosexuals in the camps. One of my uncle's colleagues remembered his 'treat' of a job: to shove huge piles of dead bodies into the ovens and burn them. The piles were so large that they had to try and burn three bodies at a time, even if the oven was only designed for one person at a time."

Lisbeth came twice to the B-CC classes, telling stories that brought to life a part of history—the nonviolent Danish resistance—that the students were quick to realize were ignored in their classrooms.

Dear Lisbeth:

I appreciate your taking time to come to our class and inform us about a significant part of history I was not aware of. It is impressive that the Danish people were able to control themselves and not only fight back with violence. It must have been difficult to resist that urge. It also makes me happy that the Danish people had the decency to warn and help the Jewish Danes, instead of sitting back to watch their neighbors be killed, as happened in many other countries.

The struggles that the Danes faced and how they responded was admirable and inspiring. Much is to be learned by their example, so I hope that you continue to tell the Denmark story.

Good luck,
Andres Wright

Dear Lisbeth:

Thank you for coming to the US to teach us about a movement that cannot be found in our history textbooks. I find it strange that our classes teach us only about the battles of World War II and its warriors but so rarely to we learn about the history of nonviolence. The Danish resistance is something to be admired and celebrated as proof that nonviolence can resolve violence.

Thank you for sharing your country's story.

Liza Brilliant

Dear Lisbeth:

As a Jew, I have learned time and again about World War II. Yet somehow, I have not learned enough about the Danish resistance. I really appreciate your enlightening us on this topic. I think the tactic of complicity with the Germans and then performing clever strikes is genius. This form of resistance saved the lives of many, many Jews, and I feel that often goes unrecognized. Thank you for taking time out of your busy schedule to come and talk to us and answer our questions.

Sincerely,
Celia Goldfarb

Dear Lisbeth:

Your visit to our class was eye-opening. We've learned about World War II in history class but never about Denmark's role. I had no idea that the Danish citizens would have peaceful protests and go on strikes. It was also fascinating to see how these peaceful protests were more effective than using violence because they stopped Nazi production. Overall, I found your visit to our class was informative, and I'm happy to learn about Denmark.

From,
Fergus

37

I F ASKED TO make a list of the helping professions, most citizens would include coaches, social workers, nurses and doctors, caddies, mediators, teachers, physical therapists, guidance counselors, lawyers, rabbis, imams, priests and nuns, bus drivers, police officers. It wouldn't be likely that financial consultants in the Charles Schwab Company would make the cut or that many people would move beyond the perception that money managers are little more than stock market gamblers in the Wall Street casinos known as the New York Stock Exchange.

They might change their minds if they met Giselle Cruz Colavita in her Schwab office at 4701 Wisconsin Avenue, Bethesda, a five-minute walk from the peace studies classrooms at B-CC where she shared her story.

A 1996 graduate of Holy Child Girls School in Potomac, Maryland, and a 2000 graduate of Gettysburg College with a French and political science degree, Giselle writes, "I lived in France in my junior year, which helped me become trilingual. My first language was Spanish at home. Shortly after college I went to work for a venture capital fund where I helped with in-house translations and research. But I quickly became much more interested in the idea of investing in businesses, ideas, and people via the stock market, the bond market, and other possibilities. This was when I decided to help people invest their money to secure a better future for themselves by investing in businesses, ideas, and people. Unfortunately there is a misconception that everyone in finance is a 'shark' due in large part to movies like *Wall Street*, *Boiler Room*, or *The Wolf of Wall Street*. What I do every day could not be further from this distortion. I help families achieve their goals in life by making sure they have the financial security to do so. I do this in large part by creating and sticking to a financial plan, making sure they are diversified, rebalancing consistently, and investing in good quality and low-cost investments."

Giselle's family immigrated from Argentina to the United States in 1972. "I was born in Holy Cross hospital in Silver Spring and grew up in the DC area. My father came to this country owing money for his plane ticket. He started from nothing. He is now seventy-eight and started [working] at nine in Argentina as a tailor's apprentice. It would become his trade. On coming to America, he worked as a janitor at Lord & Taylor in Chevy Chase. Shortly after he was an assistant to the tailor at the department store and eventually worked his way up to head tailor. He heard about a tailor shop in Rockville's congressional plaza called Sam's Tailoring. Sam hired my dad to become his head tailor. After a while, Sam wanted to retire and offered his business to my dad. Back then, small business loans were much easier to get. Combined with this loan and my dad's very hard work, he was able to buy Sam out and found himself as a business owner. He changed the name of the company to Hector's Tailoring. He would operate it for forty-plus years. My dad's realization of the 'American Dream' is what put me through school, ballet, and piano classes. I am especially proud of my dad."

Dear Giselle:

After you came to teach us about finance, I went home and tried to learn even more. I never knew much about money or stocks or saving bonds, so I talked to my mom about it all!

In one day, I learned more about money and what people do with it than I had ever known until then. So thank you for expanding my knowledge and my interest in this field. You are one smart person, and I'm glad to hear that your job makes you happy.

Sincerely,
Andrei Pinkus

Dear Giselle:

I first learned about the economy and Wall Street in honors US history during my freshman year. I always found it compelling that people could buy company shares or holdings at the cost of a dollar or so and live off it. But I think that those investors are taking huge risks into buying shares because there is always a strong possibility that the market could crash again and those who invested will lose everything.

Now that I am older and about to enter the world of adulthood, I am always thinking about how I am going to make money, saving, and paying my bills and taxes. One of my major fears on what I want to accomplish in life is not being able to provide for others. We live world that runs on money. America is a very capitalist country, and it seems that the only way many people make their way in life is becoming richer and wealthier than others—which is a sin.

I want to make my way in life by helping people and making the world a simpler, safer, and more productive environment for people to live in.

Whenever I'm struggling, I hope to find you for your guidance. I want to thank you for sharing your story and your social financial skills with us. I hope you come back again and may God be with you and your fortunes to come.

Sincerely,
Derrick Jones

Dear Giselle:

Your experiences in financial advising is fascinating, and I'm sure you've helped a lot of people secure a stable future. Thank you for sharing your thoughts on investing with our class. It's a topic we never learn about in school.

Sincerely,
Lillian Parr

Dear Giselle:

I had never thought about investing too much before your talk. I always assumed it was too risky and not worth the trouble, but you completely changed my mind. Your presentation, so poised and analytical, impressed me greatly.

The balanced portfolio you described really aroused my interest. Thank you for coming to our class. I am going to try and invest as soon as I can, and I promise to give Charles Schwab strong consideration.

Best,
Will Fusting

Dear Giselle:

Your job is so incredibly different from anything I've known! I absolutely loved getting to learn about stocks and investments. I had never been taught anything about them before.

How you ended up at your job was reassuring for me because I am totally unsure what career I want. Your ability to find one that love, even though it doesn't relate to your major, is really calming for me.

Sincerely,
Kate Strathman

38

"I 'M FROM ODESSA," Maren Lujan writes, "a small city in West Texas near the border of New Mexico. As a child, my parents traveled extensively for work or pleasure to Mexico where my family's roots are. Even though my parents weren't the wealthiest, they raised me to appreciate the value of travel and exploration. That desire to travel stuck with me throughout the years. When I learned about the Peace Corps, it seemed like the perfect fit for me.

"I first needed a degree, one that I would earn from the University of Texas, with a major in psychology and a minor in anthropology. To enroll in the Peace Corps Youth Development program, I needed work experience. For two years I labored as a college advisor in under-served high schools, both in San Antonio and Austin. Unfortunately, during my application process I was put on medical hold for a short period. In the meantime I worked as a case manager for adolescents and their families in Central Texas. Eventually Peace Corps offered a departure date for a public health position in Koliagbe, Guinea, West Africa. I accepted.

"Never having heard of Guinea, I had to Google the country to study up before leaving. I also had to deal with my family's doubts and fears of sending me so far away.

"In my family, young girls don't typically leave home until they marry. Although I had already left my hometown years back for college, somehow traveling thousands of miles away didn't compare.

My mother finally accepted that I wouldn't change my mind. On November 30, 2012, I set off.

"As a public health volunteer in a foreign country, I had to deal with navigating a new culture and language. I was forced to challenge my cultural assumptions and expectations, both for others and myself. This became my most valuable lesson.

"While I don't think my work while in Guinea had the *amazing* impact I had hoped it would, I do believe I left a more open-minded person due to my service. I feel better prepared to work as an ally and advocate within communities.

"Before leaving, many of my American friends questioned how one could 'survive' living in in West Africa, a question that seems so silly now because now I have a new understanding I didn't possess before. Although at times I'm unsure of what impact I had in my town of Koliagbe, joining the Peace Corps has been the best decision I ever made."

It is all too common for returned volunteers to pursue more education, usually a master's degree in international development. For Maren, it was American University from which she graduated after the fall semester 2016. Luckily for me, she enrolled in my "Peace and Special Justice" for which she received no credit. It was in her final weeks of school that she came one morning to speak to the B-CC peace studies class.

> Dear Maren:
>
> It was refreshing to have you come to our class and talk, for many reasons personally. First, I never heard that there was such a program that allows students to go live in another country and do all that you did. As someone who came to America at age six from Russia, I have already gone through culture shock and had similar thoughts as you had but forgot about the crazy process of adjusting to another country until you came in and spoke

You have inspired me to want to learn more and travel to another country as you did. I never knew that my interest in getting a chance to live in another culture is possible. I am really excited go learn more.

Natalie Schwartz

(Sorry for my messy handwriting. I got excited and didn't write so clearly).

Dear Maren:

Your experience in Guinea has made my idea of my future so much bigger. I never thought about what came after college, but now I have the possibility of joining the Peace Corps. You have changed people's lives in such a larger way. The families suffering in those villages had you as their support

After listening to your journey, I have decided to go and help in a Third World country and inspire people as you have. Thank you so much for coming to our class. It meant so much.

Sincerely,
Marley Clendenin

Dear Maren:

Hearing you speak about the Peace Corps just gets me even more excited for when I join. My parents were members in Poland, and I've grown up listening to their stories. I hope to go right after college. I was an exchange student in Argentina last year, and I totally get what you mean when you discussed culture shock.

Argentina's already a bit Americanized (and I was shocked), so I can imagine Guinea. You seem like you have really big things ahead of you.

Thanks,
Marisa Arsenault

39

MEG HANLON, A 1986 Phi Betta Kappa graduate from Middlebury College including a year at Yale, and earning a master's in education curriculum and instruction in 2016, has had a hand in public relations, film production, medical research, kindergarten teaching, yoga teaching, and now mediation. She is the mother of Elena de Toledo and her brother Nico who took the peace studies class before going on to Pomona College.

> Dear Meg Hanlon:
>
> My dad is a lawyer, so I've always figured that if you're mad at someone, you sue them. It wasn't until your talk that I understood that there are more peaceful, respectful ways to solve disputes.
>
> Thank you for coming to our class and educating us on your work. Mediation will be something I keep in mind next when I feel disrespected. I know I can speak for the class when I say we all learned something from your talk.
>
> Thank you.
>
> Olivia Goodman

Dear Ms. Hanlon:

My dad is a lawyer, and over the summer, I went to work with him. While there I met one of his clients who was getting a divorce from his wife. The meeting between the two of them was awful. They both ardently believed that they were right and would not listen to the other's opinion. Through seeing their interaction, I realized the importance of listening to other people and considering their thoughts. No one is ever going to be completely right or wrong, and I think your work really shows that. You help people work through their differences and come to reasonable conclusions. I admire that.

Best,
Jillian Walsh

40

IN 2012, RACHEL Moo was one of 920 students in her graduating class at Trenton, New Jersey, High School and then was to be a varsity swimmer in the 50 freestyle at Syracuse University. After a teaching fellowship at Tufts, she became a second-grade teacher at the Neighborhood House Charter school in Dorchester near Boston. Among her students was Martin Richard, an eight-year-old who appreciated Ms. Moo's peace studies class where Gandhi's line, "an eye for any eye and we all go blind," was among the many worthy ideas and ideals discussed. A few fellow teachers saw Rachel as a bit over the edge and something of an academic troublemaker for deviating from the always sacred core curriculum—and to study peace-making, no less.

She had taken her class on a field trip to a nearby peace rally at which Martin carried his hand-printed sign: No More Hurting People. Peace.

Two days before the 26.2 mile Boston Marathon, Martin ran in a relay race. He relished it so much that he was told by Rachel to keep at it, and when he reached eighteen they could run the marathon together.

At the 2013 race, Rachel went to the thronged finish line at Boylston Street to catch up with Martin and his family among the spectators. She was not in time. The Richards were standing within feet of the second bomb, an explosion that killed Martin and three others while severely injuring her parents and sister. As chaos and fury swept in, a stunned Rachel walked home to Dorchester, a three-hour grieving walk.

Not long after, and seeking to honor the memory of Martin, the thirty-seven-year-old former swimmer decided to run the 2014 marathon and soon began putting in the training miles and putting aside all self-doubts that she could go the distance. At noon on the April 21 race day, where thirty-nine thousand runners—some of them seasoned and self-confident and others first-timers bracing for the muscle aches sure to come well before the twenty-mile mark at Heartbreak Hill—left the village of Hopkinton for the trek to Boston. Wearing number 31776 on her bib and with peace printed on his yellow shirt, Rachel's time was 5:38 and 52 seconds. "I could feel Martin with me the whole time," Rachel told a reporter. "When I was struggling in the final three miles, I said to him, 'C'mon, Martin, we can't stop now, we have to get to the finish.' When I did, it was an incredible feeling. And I definitely felt Martin was crossing it with me."

> Dear Rachel:
> I still remember watching the news the day the Boston bombing happened. I couldn't take my eyes off the TV as the manhunt took place. After your talk, I found that there is another perspective to what happened that day. A rabbi at my temple was also there at the marathon and was close to the finish line when the bombs went off.
> I cannot begin to imagine what it must have been like to be there that afternoon while everything was taking place. I know it was a different type of horror from just watching it on the news.
> You have overcome a lot in your life, and I admire that about you. Thank you for everything you've done to make this world a better place.
>
> Best,
> Olivia Goodman

Dear Rachel:

Tears welled up in my eyes as you spoke of Martin's awe-inspiring legacy. Your grit and integrity have really touched me. I hope you continue to tell your story and run as many marathons as you can because you are a symbol of hope to all of us. Continue being such a blessing.

Lots of hope for the future—

Aniqa Ahmed

Dear Rachel:

Your courage and strength give me hope for a more peaceful future. What you do for Martin is pure kindness. You are helping this boy live within you. As someone who experienced a ton of loss already in my life, I understand the feelings of darkness.

I am still trying to learn to forgive but seeing someone as strong as you being able to forgive those people helps me. I hope to have passion and reason for my life like you. I want to become a nurse and change people's lives for the better as you have.

Thank you—

Marley Clendenin

41

WHILE DELIVERING A speech on Valentine's Day in Minneapolis in 1979, Ralph Neas suddenly felt wobbly, a kind of dizziness that led to the slurring of words. He had to leave the podium. He was soon in St. Mary's hospital and, near death in the ICU, about to receive the last rites from a Catholic priest. At thirty-two, he had Guillain-Barre, known as "French Polio," an illness that paralyzes the nerves and muscles and left Ralph Neas sedated for pain and unable to talk or walk for nearly five months. He credits Sister Margaret Francis Shilling for his unlikely recovery: "She was the person who saved my life, helped me spiritually and totally renewed much of my faith… Sister would come at least a couple of times a day, holding my hand and talking to me about my strange friends back in Washington."

Among those strange ones are friends that Ralph Neas had made and would make in his long decades of public service, including six years as chief of staff for Sen. Edward Brooke of Massachusetts, two years for Sen. Dave Durenberger of Minnesota, and as the head of the Leadership Conference on Civil Rights and People for the American Way. The effectiveness of his work and proven skills to join forces with both Republicans and Democrats led Sen. Ted Kennedy to describe Ralph Neas as "the 101st senator for civil rights."

A 1968 graduate of the University of Notre Dame and three years from the University of Chicago Law School, he married Katherine Beh in 1988. She had been on the staff of Sen. Tom Harkin of Iowa. Before speaking to the peace studies class, he was introduced by his daughter Maria whose love and admiration for her illustrious father was fully evident.

Dear Mr. Neas:

When you told us that you were a white Catholic Republican* heading an organization devoted to civil rights, I was surprised. That seems like a demographic that would be opposed to civil rights. But you're not, and that makes me happy. You're right that we need to compromise in these times to get things done. I just hope that compromise can come before it's too late.

Sincerely,
Cicelie Gray

*Ralph Neas left the Republican party in 1970 to join the Democrats.

Dear Mr. Neas:

I was holding my breath during your speech, waiting for you to get political and for the Trump supporters in the room to erupt. But you expertly appealed to bipartisan ideologies, speaking out without offending anyone. So thank you so much for speaking with truth and logic. And thank you for giving us Democrats in the room a little bit of hope and restore faith in the political system.

Sincerely,
Rebecca Schrader

Dear Mr. Neas:

I was intrigued by your talk. It was refreshing to hear about cross-party politics and bipartisan work. We as a society have much to learn from your hard work and determination to have us all get along. We need more politicians like you to be willing to work on and on behalf of both sides of the aisle. As someone who plans to pursue government, politics and/or law, your recollections about the cooperation and goodness in government was uplifting.

I was especially impressed to hear about your role in standing up against a conservative Supreme Court nominee [Robert Bork]. On behalf of everyone who benefitted from the same-sex-marriage decision, Planned Parenthood, and voting rights, thank you.

Sincerely,
Cate Paterson

Dear Dad:

I was so grateful to have had you come speak in peace studies. It touching to see you captivate seventy students. Many came up to me and said how awesome you are. You have such a natural ability to capture people's attention and really engage them in what you're talking about.

Thank you for taking time out of your days to do so. Me, Mr. McCarthy, and my peers appreciate it. I am super lucky to have you for a dad. Thanks for being the best. You should come back anytime.

Love you,
Maria

42

I N 2000, SHORTLY after earning a degree from Swarthmore College and several years after graduating from Bethesda-Chevy Chase High School in 1993, Theresa Williamson was working on a doctorate in city planning at the University of Pennsylvania that she would earn in 2004. The daughter of a British father and Brazilian mother who were living and working in Bethesda, Theresa was residing part-time in Rio de Janeiro as the founding director of Catalytic Communities.

The purpose of the nonprofit is to provide media and networking support to families in Rio's favelas. One news story described Theresa: "She is an outspoken and respected advocate on behalf of Rio's favelas to help ensure that they are recognized for their heritage status and their residents fully served as equal citizens."

Before visiting favela neighborhoods as part of her PhD dissertation research, Theresa had the common misconceptions that favelas were sprawling scenes of fetid slum violence, crimes, and chaos that should be bulldozed into oblivion. Little time on the ground was needed for Theresa to see the other side, the true side, and realize that favelas "are probably the most stigmatized urban communities in the world. What I found," she told an interviewer from Guernica in 2016, "were basically communities working hard and self-organizing to manage and respond to all sorts of local challenges, whether it was fixing sewage systems, housing, day-care programs, after-school programs, soccer programs, dental hygiene, cooperatives—basically any social, environmental challenge you can think of. These were communities actively addressing those challenges."

In my peace studies class, Theresa was committed both ethically and politically to animal rights, a stand that took her well beyond a vegan diet. She was a regular protestor at the Gartenhaus fur store at 7101 Wisconsin Avenue where the mannequins were gussied up in the hides of minks, silvers foxes, chinchillas, and assorted big cats.

> Dear Theresa:
>
> I'd heard about Brazil and its favelas being extremely dangerous and inefficient. But I never heard about their creativity and efficiency in creating communities without government help. It's really sad we're only shown the bad things about favelas, tainting our judgment of them. I had no idea they were amazing in so many ways: their infrastructure, committees, economy, and most importantly, their communities. These people have been forgotten by the government, and instead of sulking in hatred toward politicians, they build their lives and create their own communities.
>
> Thank you for informing us on both sides of the issue. I never would've known favelas were so fantastic.
>
> Keep on working hard!
>
> Maria Villegas

> Dear Ms. Williamson:
>
> Thank you for opening my eyes yesterday. Before you spoke with our class, I knew virtually nothing about the cultural and political climate in Rio, let alone favelas. I had heard of them before, but I knew little about what they are or why they are so important.

Learning about the vibrancy and creative beauty these communities have was incredible. Without hearing the real story behind favelas, I would have assumed they were poor slums of Rio, just as how the rest of the world seems to view them.

I am so grateful to have had the opportunity to listen to you and hear the truth about favelas and the situation in Rio. We need more people like you to educate the general public and put to rest these misconceptions so we can have a more peaceful and less judgmental world.

Thank your teaching me about favelas, it really opened my eyes.

Sincerely,
Elizabeth Mulvihill

Dear Theresa:

I've been to Brazil, and I see what you mean about how, with a little structure, vibrancy can erupt.

I think it's amazing the work you've been doing, and I really appreciate how you let favela leaders decide what their communities need and train them in achieving their goals. I'm interested in South America. I did an exchange program in Argentina, and during college I plan to take a gap year to Brazil. I'm curious about your nonprofit. I would love to intern with you at some point.

Muito obrigado!

Marisa Arsenault

Dear Theresa:

The way you've decided to live your life is incredible. It's inspiring that you've used your education to help better other people's lives, especially in a place that so few people pay attention to. Your work is clearly important and effective. It's amazing that you've dedicate your career to it.

Thank you so much for showing us how unexpected life can be. It's reassuring to hear from someone who's been in the exact same place as us.

Sincerely,
Kate Strathmann

43

T HE YEAR AFTER Bob Schlehuber graduated from the University of Illinois in 2008 with a BA in communication, he found himself teaching 250 boys in School Number 7 in Pryvilla, a coal town of ten thousand in eastern Ukraine. He was a Peace Corps volunteer. He started a basketball team, an environmental club, and organized a student-run school newspaper. His monthly Peace Corps stipend was twenty dollars, his apartment thirty dollars a month. To his credit, he used his in-country training to learn Russian, the better to communicate with his students and their families.

Before leaving Pryvillya in 2011, Bob created a national training program that offered free social and educational lessons to all of Ukraine. "The program," he recalls, "trained over one thousand teachers throughout the country at no cost. It has given me energy to continue to create projects that promote peace building."

Many more than his students came to appreciate Bob's outreach. His service, said Doug Teschner, the Peace Corps Ukraine country director, "was especially notable as he showed such wide range versatility, a truly special gift for volunteers to acquire early in their service. Robert's work was one of great uniqueness and made me proud to serve as his country director."

From Rockford, Illinois, near the Wisconsin border, Bob came to Washington to earn a master's in Peace and Conflict Resolution from American University's School of International Service.

Generously, he has been a regular in my B-CC classes. He uses the opening minutes of his visits to ask each student to say their name and which social issue they most care about.

> Dear Bob:
>
> Your arrival to our class couldn't have been more perfectly timed. I just returned from my soon-to-be college, UNC Chapel Hill and have been trying to pick a major. I've been leaning toward global studies and was intrigued by the idea of the Peace Corps. Hearing you share your story and how much you learned while you were in Ukraine was fascinating.
>
> Your passion for bridging cultures is crucial for society, especially now as we fear the unknown with our new commander in chief. I so admire your bravery and courage to go live in a totally foreign environment and learn a whole new language. I love to travel, but the idea of two years and a whole new language is definitely daunting but also exciting.
>
> Thank you so much for taking the time to come in and talk with us but also wanting to get to know us. You're the first speaker to ask us our names.
>
> I wish you the best in the future.
>
> Many thanks—
>
> Sarah Payne

> Dear Bob:
>
> I've learned in my last years in high school that change, especially social change, starts with each of us. This made your visit so encouraging. You showed us that if you are passionate for something, you can make a difference, and there

is always something you can do to help people, from the Peace Corps to your peace building organization. Hearing you draw out a passion for social change from every one of us gave me so much hope that this is generation that will create lasting change.

It was great to hear what my classmates are passionate about, and it showed me that none of us are alone in our fight for social justice. I don't actually know all my classmates too well, but you cemented each of them in my mind as allies in the long fight ahead (with a new president in office).

Thank you not only for speaking to our class but also for your years of volunteering and peace building, which has surely given my generation a leg up in the fight for change. You have inspired me to never stop working for what I cannot accept, so thank you.

Cate Paterson

Dear Bob Schlehuber:

I strongly agree with the purpose of your work to bring people together through culture. On a personal level, I have seen that happen to myself and it has changed my life. I am Japanese, and as you may know, the east Asian countries of China, Korea, and Japan have a culturally close but politically complicated relationship.

Last year, I got into Korean pop music, and I spend a substantial—perhaps too much so— amount of time listening to music in a language I don't understand, investing emotions in the historical drama of a country that isn't my own, and obsessing over artists who fit un-American and even un-Japanese beauty standards. I even convinced my parents to take me to Korea where it saddened me to see the memorials all over the place basically saying "there was this beautiful historic thing until the Japanese came and destroyed it in that XYZ occupation. Thank God the Americans were there for us."

I am Japanese American, but I have come to realize there is no need to overcomplicate things. I don't listen to music as an American or Japanese. I listen to music as an individual, and the culture I enjoy just happens to come from Korea. It is important to carry the history of my nationalities, but hopefully the free exchange of cultural exports will give a more promising future to friendships between countries.

Mian Osumi

44

F ROM 1975 TO the early 2000s, Bernie Survil, well into his years
as a Roman Catholic priest, was offering acts of solace and dis-
pensing the sacraments to mostly impoverished communities in El
Salvador, Guatemala, Nicaragua, and Costa Rica. Those were the
imperiled times when Central American Catholicism was a church of
martyrs, when bishops like Oscar Romero, Jesuit priests, Maryknoll
nuns, and thousands of laity were routinely slain by death squads. It
was when Ronald Reagan and his lackeys like Alexander Haig, Elliott
Abrams, and Oliver North were supplying weapons and money to
dictators—all in the name of stopping communism.

Servil came close to joining the death list when government
goons in El Salvador came to his church one afternoon. He was
arrested, blindfolded, and knocked to the ground but eventually
released. Days later, he recalls, "I was kidnapped at the point of a gun
at night in from of my home and driven into Guatemala and turned
over to armed men in a jeep who could have been an execution gang,
but rather I was jailed, accused of being in Guatemala illegally, and
deported. I was spared, for sure, because I was an American citizen."

Little of this was in Survil's aspirations when ordained in 1967
and looking forward to a comfortable life as a parish priest in conservative Western Pennsylvania. As the death toll of the Vietnam
war grew and grew, far more for the Vietnamese than Americans,
Survil began condemning US foreign policy. His bishop told him to
clam up, stick to his sacerdotal chores, and quit the agitations. Survil

didn't, and when he left to work in Central America, his bishop was "very happy" to have him gone.

In 2003, having been jailed in Central America for troublemaking, Survil now found himself jailed by the Bush administration. His crime? Trespassing at Fort Benning, Georgia, where he was among thousands protesting the US Army's School of the Americas where the juntas soldiers were trained in the arts of killing, which they ably practiced on returning home. Every third weekend in November for more than twenty-five years, thousands of protestors, organized by Roy Bourgeois, a Navy veteran and former priest, have gathered at the Fort Benning gates calling for the School of the Americas—better known as the School of Assassins—to be closed. War-funding Congresses have consistently refused.

For crossing the line, Servil was sentenced to three months in federal prison. Among those who also trespassed was Jack Gilroy, a high school social studies teacher in Endwell, New York. Something of a recidivist, he has also done time for antiwar protests at other military bases.

In the July 15, 2016, *National Catholic Reporter*, Gilroy told the chilling story of Ben Salmon, a pacifist from Denver who refused to be drafted to fight in World War I: "He opposed the war as immoral, as an abuse of political power and he firmly opposed the Catholic held theory of just war. The war was not in conformity with his belief in the nonviolent Christ… He was sentenced first to death and then to a reduced sentence of 25 years of hard labor." Shackled, he was shuffled and to and from seven federal prisons during his journey of mistreatment, and often kept in solitary confinement, once over a fetid sewer with hungry rats. Government prosecutors, unable to break Salmon, decided that his pacifist stands were clearly signs of mental illness sent him to Washington's St. Elizabeths Hospital for the insane. Under pressure from the ACLU and a professor from Catholic University, the secretary of war in the Wilson administration eventually released Salmon in 1920.

That story, among others, was one that Gilroy told the B-CC peace studies classes. He shared the time with Bernie Survil.

Dear Bernie and Jack:

I have known several "delinquents" in my relatively short life (my father and post-hippie housemate are two for you). By "delinquents," I mean those who have had several rough run-ins with the law. Don't take this the wrong way, but you two are by far the most peculiar and intriguing pair I have ever met: a high school social studies teacher and a pastor. Sure, sure. A gruff, foreign car-loving Long Island man with a propensity for speeding (my father) and jittery, pot-smoking Californian with leanings to flipping off police are not surprising figures to see in the slammer, but you two have defied *all* conventions. I am so proud to know you!

In all seriousness, you two have demonstrated admirable dedication to all your ideals. You not only have peaceful beliefs, but you have applied them to your personal lives—a refreshing change from the general hypocrisy of people who cry about their impotence when asked to fully act on their principles.

Bernie, you protested against the School of the Americas, sentenced to prison, and now endure a stigma by the church hierarchy—simply because you stood up for what you believe in.

Jack, you snuck into the School of the Americas and were forced to serve a sentence in a high security prison—again, simply because you stood up for what you believed in.

You both took on the violent culture that the United States perpetuates and reinforces in other countries, breeding its own destruction and most importantly the destruction of others. Further, you challenged the voluntary ignorance much of the public maintains when the government's injustice and despicable ethics are exposed.

Thank you for your witness and remaining loyal to your beliefs. You both have been, and continue to be, remarkably courageous and resolute. Hopefully, I can do the same when I need to defend my morals.

Thank you for speaking.

Sincerely,
Elizabeth Stephens

Dear Bernie and Jack:

I always used to think those who ended up in jail for protesting were violent rebels who had a fierce cause but were unwilling to go about it peacefully. You have both shown me how incorrect I was in that assumption.

The way you tote your inmate IDs with you wherever you go is not only hilarious, but representative of how proud you both are of your unconditional work for peace. It is inspiring. It reminds me of the quote: "He who has strong enough why can bear almost any kind of how." I want to be in front of students one day, telling stories of all the risks I took to do better.

Thank you for your fight—

Sabine Rundlet

Dear Bernie and Jack:

I think in the end that even though institutions such as schools encourage innovation and questioning, in reality no authority—though it may be expected—actually wants you to protest. Though the government touts freedom and liberty, as soon as both of you exercised your right to protest (and for humanitarian ideals at that) you were thrown into jail.

Ultimately, if you choose to work within the system as a politician, you have to compromise somewhere, especially on foreign policy. The two politicians I see no compromise in (or very little) are Elizabeth Warren and Bernie Sanders. Especially Senator Sanders who has delved in the Israeli-Palestine conflict.

Thank you for you service to this country.

Mian Osumi

Dear Bernie and Jack:

To be honest, if I saw either of you walking down the street, I would never think that you had been arrested and put in jail multiple times. You also changed the way that I see Catholics, as you are both men of faith as well as rebels. Now I know that the only way to enact change is to take risks. You have both taken serious risks, but it seems they've all been worthwhile because you're still fighting for justice.

I'm not accustomed to learning about alternatives to violence, but your talks have inspired me to do more exploring as well as soul searching so that I may also commit myself to a noble cause.

Thank you for sharing your stories.

Sincerely,
Isabel Brown

Acknowledgments

F OR STARTERS, I'M grateful to Paul and Annie Mahon for their generosity and friendship in supporting my teaching at Bethesda-Chevy Chase High School. For five years now, they have funded Peacemaker Awards of three thousand dollars to each of sixgraduating seniors whose commitments to nonviolence were both genuine and effective. I was pleased to have had the Mahon's daughter Hanna in my class at Wilson High School before she went on to Middlebury College.

Since 1985, when my wife, Mavourneen, and I founded the Center for Teaching Peace, one of the earliest and consistent supporters of our nonprofit was the Helen Sperry Lea Foundation. As our work became better known, it would be joined by the Jack Olender Foundation, the Florence and John Schumann Foundation, the National Student Leadership Conference, the Lubsen Charitable Gift Foundation, the Washington Post Company, the El-Hibri Charitable Foundation, the Lichtmman Family Trust, the Barbra Streisand Foundation, the Morris and Gwendolyn Cafritz Foundation, the Nuclear Age Peace Foundation, the Nicholas B. Ottoway Foundation, the Public Welfare Foundation, and the Penny and Ray Watts Trust.

Through the good fortune of personal contacts, I'm grateful for the support of Dr. Laura Christianson, Liz Wenger, Katherine Hessler, Tommy Boone, John Storhm, Barbara Zimmerman, Maryanne Burke, Jim Monahan, Dr. Arthur Milholland, Dr. Lucille Mostello, Tara Foran, Joanne Kim, Amr Farouki, Bernard Demszuk, Baron Perlman, Joan Baez, Linda Smith, James Otis, Clair Nader, Ralph Nader, Jim McGovern, Nathaniel Mills, Susan See, Morton

Mintz, Claudia Levy, Tom Stewart, Anna Karavangelos, Grace Kelly, Richard DeBona, Ayiesha Alizai Sadik, Rep. Marci Kaptur, Ruth Sherer and Charles Stevenson, and others of spirited nature.

To them and others of spirited natures, my thanks for keeping faith with the ideal that increasing peace and decreasing violence is not only possible but probable—if we buck the headwinds, starting today. Tomorrow is too late.

About the Author

HAILED AS "AMERICA'S Professor Peace" by the *Los Angeles Times*, Colman McCarthy took to the classrooms in 1982 to teach the literature of peace and the methods of practical conflict resolution. Whether on the adjunct faculty at Georgetown Law School, American University, the University of Maryland, Georgetown, Oak Hill Prison, and Bethesda Chevy Chase High School, he has had more than twenty thousand students in his classes.

Ending in 1997, he was a columnist for nearly thirty years at *The Washington Post*. His books include *All of One Peace*, *I'd Rather Teach Peace*, and *Inner Companions*. He is the director of the Center for Teaching Peace, a Washington nonprofit supported by some of America's most progressive foundations. A pacifist and vegetarian, he commutes more than two thousand miles a year by bicycle.

When honored in 2014 for "Outstanding Teaching" by American University, a student praised him as "by far the most impressive professor I had had the opportunity to meet. Professor McCarthy has this amazing ability to challenge the way we see the world. He has influenced the lives of thousands through his teaching of nonviolent conflict resolution. He has changed the world for the better. I can only dream to someday change the lives of every person I meet as Professor McCarthy has changed mine."

CPSIA information can be obtained
at www.ICGtesting.com
Printed in the USA
FFHW020646030319
50778370-56205FF

9 781644 242346